SCIFs
and
Synchronicities

This book is dedicated to my family.

FOREWORD

A SCIF (pronounced 'skiff') is, in U. S. security and intelligence parlance, a Sensitive Compartmented Information Facility. A SCIF is a 'lock-up' where Top Secret work is done.

Synchronicities - those mysterious and, at the time, unexplainable things that occur against seemingly impossible odds. Synchronicities are different from coincidences, in that they have a special meaning to the observer.

TABLE OF CONTENTS

So how best to tell my stories, and about the amazing synchronicities that seem to tie my life together?

I could start at the beginning of my life and proceed chronologically, but that might not be so interesting – first I did this, then I did that, etc.

I can remember the times my paternal grandfather would sit back in his rocking chair and tell whatever story from his past came to his mind. He'd put his hands together, almost in a prayerful position, and 'twiddle' his thumbs as he rocked back and forth.

Let me take you on my grandfather's kind of trip about my life - not necessarily in chronological order - but as things come to mind, and as they seem to be related in my life experience.

Let's get some basic facts out of the way. I was born in Middletown, Ohio, on July 1st, 1939. I know because my mother happened to be there at the time.

I'm in the highchair. My mother, Dorothy, is feeding me. On my left are my maternal great grandparents, William and Frances ("Fanny") Whitehead. My dad, Homer Leffler, is carving the turkey. On his right is my maternal great-grandfather Ben Francis from Lyons, France. On Dad's immediate left are my maternal grandparents, Ada and 'Les' Francis. Next to Grandpa Francis are my paternal grandparents, Stella and William Leffler.

I was nicknamed "Mick" by Grandma Francis. When I was a baby, she said I looked like a little (Irish) 'Mick'.

I started smoking at an early age,
but Grandpa Francis made me give him back his pipe after the photograph was taken.

I grew up in Middletown, and went to college in New York, Indiana, Michigan, and Florida. I've worked in Florida, Nevada, and California. I now live in Ventura, California with my wife, Holley Gene.

I spent my first fours years living (with my mom and dad) in a ground floor apartment next to the funeral home where my dad worked.

My dad, Homer Durbin Leffler, was a partner with an older man, Walter N. McCoy. The McCoy-Leffler Funeral Home was located at the corner of Broad Street and First Street in Middletown, Ohio (Middletown - so-named because Middletown is located halfway between Dayton and Cincinnati, Ohio).

Half a block up Broad Street, toward the city's center, was the town's bowling alley. What fun it was to go watch folks bowl! On summer evenings, the bowling alley opened their windows (there was no air conditioning back then) and from our front porch I could hear the pins being knocked over.

I wasn't allowed to sit out front all that much because First and Broad was a busy corner. Also, the city bus station was on Broad St., across from the bowling alley. There were a lot of buses turning that corner and a lot of dirty exhaust fumes.

The funeral home was kitty-cornered from The Middletown Journal (newspaper) building, and across the street from St. Paul's Evangelical and Reformed Church that my family and I attended while I lived in Middletown.

Our minister, Rev. Harold Jung (pronounced like 'young'), lived a few houses down on Broad Street from us and across the street from the church.

Rev. Jung picked up extra money by coming over to our house and cutting my dad's and my hair.

I liked Rev. Jung – and I especially liked his daughter, Marna. Marna and I played together.

Another playmate was a boy named Ted Turner. Ted lived in Cincinnati, Ohio. Ted's mother and my mother were friends, so they would come to Middletown to visit now and then.

One time I heard Ted's mother say to him, "Why can't you be a good boy like Mickey Leffler?"

I lost track of Ted after a few visits. I never gave much thought about it until years later when I heard the name "Ted Turner" in the news.

I 'Googled' Ted Turner and discovered that we are about the same age (within 8 months) – and that he was born in Cincinnati (!!!) Ted Turner owns more land than anybody else in the country - greater than the land areas of Delaware and Rhode Island combined. He was also married to Jane Fonda.

Was the Ted Turner they were talking about the same Ted Turner I had played with as a child?

When I was about four years old, my loving sister, Barbara, was born.

We then moved to the 'East End' of town, into a two-story (plus attic) house across the street from where the high school football games were played. I never had to buy a ticket to see the games. All I had to do was climb into the attic and watch out the attic window. I could see everything.

The games were held on Friday night. On Saturday morning, I would go over and look under the bleacher seats for money that had accidently dropped out of the pockets of those attending the game. I also collected empty cigarette packs so I could remove and save the aluminum foil inside.

My Grandmother Francis recycled aluminum foil during WWII.

4

Rev. Jung was still cutting my hair.

Coincidentally, the football field was on the same property as Lincoln Elementary School, where I attended grades 1 through 6. Wow - I lived across the street from my school!

My Bicycles

I rode my bicycle everywhere. I had to. I had no car, wasn't old enough to drive anyway.

My first bike was an old one that had been repainted black. Ugly! But it worked. I rode it all around town.

Then Dad got me a new Schwinn, complete with white wall tires, a big shock absorber just below the handle bars, and an electric horn. Just push the button on the side of the 'body' (don't know what else to call it), and the horn would sound – not very loudly. Wasn't of much practical use, but, hey, it was a horn!

My dad trotted it out onto Arlington Avenue in front of our house. Then he got on it – BACKWARDS!

He rode it down the street backwards, too!

I could never do that. I didn't even try.

Guess Dad just wanted to show off.

Dad loved bicycles. Years later, he died riding one in a parade.

My bike had everything – playing cards that flapped up against the wheel spokes to make a sort of motor sound. Everything. Even had a headlight for riding at night. Didn't provide much light - especially when the batteries got 'low' – but, hey, it was cool!

I thought, "Wouldn't be great if my bike had a radio on it – just like a car!"

5

There were 'portable' radios back then. They weren't small. They ran on several big batteries needed to heat up the electronic vacuum tubes inside. The radios were big – like three big boxes of Wheaties scotch-taped together.

'Gramps' (my maternal grandfather) had an old portable radio.

I took it out of its case. Gramps helped me build a new case for it out in his 'barn' (a lot of houses in town – especially in the older neighborhoods – had large garages, left over from the horse and buggy days).

The new case was cool. No radio dial – just a big grey knob to tune to different stations, and another smaller one for volume. No speaker either – we built a speaker box and mounted it up on the handlebars. It had an on/off switch, too.

Everything fit on the Schwinn pretty well. But something was missing.

A car radio antenna!

Gramps took me down to the Western Auto store where we found a good one.

Now my bicycle was complete!

Grade School

The first day of first grade I reported to Mrs. Tyson's class. The next day, I was transferred to Miss Beacom's class. I didn't know why until a few days later. It was because I played with Freddie Tyson nearly every day (the Tysons lived on my street). Perhaps my being a student of Mrs. Tyson was against the rules at the time.

I grew up with Freddie, even playing in the Middletown Civic Symphony together in later years – he played trombone and I played bass viol (acoustic bass).

I remember two significant events in Miss Beacom's 1st grade class:

- I learned to make butter.

- I figured out my first big word. Miss Beacom wrote it on the blackboard. She said it was made up of words and sounds we already knew. The word was 'inbetween.' I was the first one in class to figure it out.

Second grade with Mrs. Evans: I remember having to learn cursive writing.

The other thing I remember about 2nd grade was that a student from one of the higher grades visited our class to draw a cartoon figure on our blackboard. Wow – he was good. Can't remember what cartoon figure he drew.

Oh, yeah, I almost forgot. One day in class, I got the idea to ask everyone in the second grade (two classrooms) to come over to my house and watch some cartoons. I had recently been given a small, toy movie projector and loved playing with it.

I forgot, however, to tell Mom and Dad I had invited both classrooms.

Fortunately, Mrs. Evans called Mom to confirm the invitation.

Neither Mom or Dad got upset. Dad went out and rented a sound movie projector and some cartoons and 'shorts' (short story movies). Mom popped a laundry basket full of popcorn. All the kids came over and we had a great time!

I cut our grass with a push mower in the summertime (no gas-powered mowers for homes back then). I thought it would be a good idea if I cut the grass at a neighbor's house to make some money. I went up the street and knocked on the neighbor's door. Yes, they'd be happy to pay me to cut their grass! I cut the front and back yards, pulled out weeds, and raked up the clippings. They gave me 50 cents!

I was so proud, I took it home and showed it to my mom. She made me take it back to them. That was too much money! I returned it like Mom said.

Third and fourth grades were a little less memorable. I do remember having to leave the third grade for a month. I had asthma and hay fever and, that year, the pollen count was very high in the Miami River Valley where I lived. Dad drove Mom and me up north to Sault St. Marie, Michigan, where the pollen count was very low. Mom and I spent the next month in a room in a tourist home, until the first snow back in Ohio.

My remembrances of that trip to Michigan:

- There was a store named Pinnacle Pete's on Spruce Street. Mom let me buy balsa wood model airplane gliders there. Once, I even got to purchase a flying model with a rubber band wind-up motor and propeller.

- The other thing was Mom and I going out to a small neighborhood restaurant. The restaurant had a jukebox that played "Peg of My Heart" performed by the Harmonicats, a popular music group at the time. I loved that song. It's interesting that several years later, my younger sister 'Peggy' was born.

With Barbara and Peggy - 1952

8

After I got home from Michigan, I did a dumb thing. Our front porch had a couple of 'jumping-off places".

I used to jump off the front porch a lot – until my feet started to hurt – a lot.

Mom took me to a 'bone doctor'. Dr. Judy found that I had broken a bone in each heel.

I had to wear elevated heel shoes for a year while the bones healed.

Another Dr. Judy, this time when I was an adult in California, played an important role in my rehabilitation after surgery. His surname wasn't spelled 'Judy' (it was Scandinavian), but he anglicized it so people could pronounce it.

Herman J. Kopp

I learned to play the bass viol in the Lincoln Elementary School orchestra – after first learning to play the bass drum. The orchestra leader was Herman J. Kopp, who I will always remember.

Several years later, after Mr. Kopp had retired (and gotten a bit older), he appeared at our side door (we rarely used the front door). I was in high school at the time. I invited him in.

Mr. Kopp was wearing a long black overcoat and a black hat.

Years later, there was a TV show called "Laugh-In." Remember the dirty old man who used to ask, "How about a Walnetto?"

Mr. Kopp looked like that.

He said to me, "I want you always to remember this song." Then he put his lips together to make the sound

9

of a trumpet. The song he 'trumpeted' was "My Bonnie Lassie."

When he was done 'trumpeting', he turned around and shuffled back outside (through our side door).

Because of his visit, I always have remembered "My Bonnie Lassie."

Maple Leaf Rag

I loved playing the piano.

My mother, Dorothy, played the piano. As a matter of fact, she studied at the Dayton, Ohio Conservatory of Music. And she played piano on the radio. She had a program called 'Dot and Dash.' 'Dot' was a nickname for Dorothy. Don't know who 'Dash' (her male partner on the program) was.

My mother, Dorothy

Mom could play "Maple Leaf Rag" like nobody's business!

Mom wanted so much for me to learn to play the piano. She tried to teach me herself at home, but it wasn't working.

Finally, she sent me to take piano lessons from Monna Conn, a dear friend of hers.

Every spring, my piano teacher, Mrs. Conn to me, would put on a piano recital. It was held in my home town's "Girls Club", a nice, large 'home' that gave room and board to young women who needed a place to stay. One feature of the home was a large hall with a stage – and a baby grand piano.

Lowell Woodrey, about my age, was another piano student of Mrs. Conn. Lowell lived in Trenton, Ohio, a small town nearby. He played very well, and later on, turned professional.

Lowell could play Mozart's Fantasie Impromptu. I could not. (Lowell was kind of like another Mr. Aronoff to me. I'll tell you about Mr. Aronoff later).

Every spring was 'nail biting time':

- I had to learn and memorize a solo. Each year Mrs. Conn ensured it would be more challenging.
- I had to learn a duet number so I could play with Lowell. He always got the 'treble' part (the higher notes on the keyboard). I always got the 'basso' part.

One Spring recital, my solo was this semi-difficult piece of music. It had a lot of 'runs' up the keyboard.

To my great dismay, as I was nearing the end of performing the piece, I noticed there was a huge spider sitting on a note at the top of the piano keyboard – the very last note I had to play in the song (!!!)

What would you have done?

Besides playing for myself, I played for others. In my high school years, I accompanied vocalists and vocal students. The vocal teacher in my hometown was also a friend of my mother. These vocalists and students sang in churches, at social functions, and in state vocal competitions. Two of these vocalists were Gibby Egleston and Sandy Minor.

Gibby was the son of my later boss at ARMCO Steel's open-hearth furnace. Gibby's mother played the organ at my dad's funeral home after I left town for college.

Gibby, a young, virile, adult male, sounded like Mario Lanza! My favorite of the songs he sang was "There Is A Balm In Gilead".

Sandy Minor, a vocal student, was a little older than I was. Sandy entered a state vocal competition and asked me to accompany her on the piano. Sandy sang "I Walked Today Where Jesus Walked".

At the end of her song, the judge rose to his feet, addressed the audience, and said, "That was one of the best performances I have been privileged to enjoy."

More exclamation marks. (!!!) I felt proud to have been her accompanist.

I finally learned to play "Maple Leaf Rag," not as well or as fast as my mother.

My daughter Heather studied piano for a while, and – guess what – she learned to play "Maple Leaf Rag", too!

My First Job

At the age of twelve, I worked at my first-ever job – at Chautauqua (pronounced 'shah – tah – kwa'). Chautauqua was a small community near the Miami River that offered rental cabins during the summer months. There was a roller skating rink, a bowling alley, meeting pavilions, and places to stay for a week at a time.

Chautauqua was managed in the summer months by Ms. Orr, who was the Principal of Lincoln Elementary School in Middletown. She helped me apply for my Social Security Card.

My 'jobs' at Chautauqua:

- I would take a key from the office and ride my bike to unlock a rental cabin for prospective tenants to inspect. I'd stay there while they looked around, then lock up and take the key back to the office.

- Chautauqua had a small bowling alley with 'duck' pins (slightly smaller than regulation-size bowling pins). The bowling balls were smaller too. This was before pin-setting machines had been invented. My job was to sit on a perch, located over and in back of the set-up pins. After the first ball was bowled, I would jump down, pick up the knocked-over pins, then return the ball to the bowler. After the last ball, I would set up the pins again for the next new frame.

My pin-setting buddies, all about my age, would sometimes set the pins up in a way to favor a cute girl bowler – maybe even not setting up the last row of pins. Sometimes, we'd set the pins up in a way to reduce the score of a loudmouthed guy. Sneaky, huh?

I learned to roller skate that summer. Oh, sure, I had learned to skate at home. My sister Barbara and I had 'sidewalk skates' that fit onto our shoes. But at the Chautauqua rink, you had to wear shoe skates with wooden wheels.

There was always someone playing the organ as the skaters went round and round the rink. I tried, but could never quite learn to skate backwards. Seems like everyone else could, though.

Chautauqua had a small general store which sold food, supplies, magazines, etc. One day I picked up an interesting-looking magazine there called *QST*. It was the first time in my life I picked up a magazine and had absolutely no idea of what it was about!

I thumbed through the pages, looked at the ads, scanned some of the articles – and still didn't have the faintest clue.

I bought the magazine and took it back to our cabin to read (Mom, my sister Barbara, and I were vacationing in Chautauqua that summer).

QST magazine was my introduction to the hobby of 'ham' radio (amateur radio).

In my junior high and high school years, I became very interested in amateur radio and learned a lot about radio and electronics.

PS: I visited Chautauqua again in 2012. It's still there.

Steam Calliope

Dad was Chairman of the Middletown Chamber of Commerce one year. He wanted to put on a parade down Central Avenue in Middletown. Dad loved parades. Sadly, he died years later while participating in one.

One of Dad's favorite songs was "Red Wing."

He had the crazy idea that I should play "Red Wing" on a steam calliope in the parade!

We went to a nearby farm and looked at a functioning steam calliope that the farmer had stored for several years in his barn.

Yep! It happened. I played "Red Wing" down Central Avenue, all the way through town - with each note of the song spitting steam and water from the pipes in my face.

Crazy, huh? But it made Dad happy.

Oh, yeah - another story about Dad and parades.

Dad had a kilt made from fabric having the plaid of the Cochran clan (Cochran - his family heritage). He marched in a parade with a (fake) bagpipe playing "Amazing Grace."

Grandma and Grampa Francis

I spent a lot of time with my maternal grandparents. Mother was their only child. That made my sisters and me their only grandchildren. They lived on Harrison Street, a half dozen or so blocks from my home on Arlington Ave. I'd ride my bike to their house, traveling most of the way through alleys.

I stayed overnight with them a lot. Grandma (her name was 'Ada') taught me how to play card games – nothing serious, just games like Canasta and 'Steal-Pile Casino' (??!).

'Gramps' (Frank Leslie Francis – everyone called him 'Les') used to work at my hometown's steel mill when he was younger. He had big arm muscles. That's who I got my middle name from – Francis. My son and my grandson, Tyler, have carried on this tradition.

In his later years, he worked as a movie theater projectionist. He became the union's lead projectionist in town. Because of this, he would visit all the theaters – even work in several different ones:

- Gordon Theater – the old Gordon caught on fire and nearly burned to the ground. I was too young to ever see a show there.

  They built a new Penneys store on the old Gordon Theater site. J.C. Penney himself attended the store's grand opening. I was there and Mr. Penney gave me a shiny new copper penny!

- Sorg Theater – the oldest theater in town, opened in 1891 as the Sorg Opera House.

- The Family Theater – a small theater down by the train tracks. You could feel it every time a train went by. I saw a lot of Abbott and Costello movies there.

- Paramount Theater – the first theater in town to
  - get a CinemaScope-sized screen
  - get a magnetic (hi-fi) sound track playback capability
  - show a 3D movie - "The House of Wax" starring Vincent Price. I saw this with Mom. Scary.

I also saw the re-release of "King Kong" with Mom at the Paramount. Scary.

In its earlier days during WWII, the Paramount hosted live stage shows with Disney characters promoting 'Buy War Bonds'. As a kid, I saw several of these shows with Mom.

Before my time, the Paramount featured a theater organ which accompanied every silent film.

I went to the Paramount often. The ticket-taker lady knew who I was and always let me in for free. I'd go upstairs to the projection booth and watch movies out its observation window. I had to wear earphones in the booth because of the noise made by the projectors.

- The Strand Theater – I went there every Saturday morning to see cartoons like Porky Pig and Bugs Bunny, 'serials' like "Rocket Man", and western films.

I Want to be a Cowboy

My favorite cowboys were Roy Rogers and Gene Autry. I liked it when Roy Rogers sang with the Sons of the Pioneers – and when he and Dale Evans sang about making " . . . the San Fernando Valley" their home. Little did I know at the time that I'd move to California some day and live near and work in the San Fernando Valley!

I also liked it when Gene Autry sang with the Riders of the Purple Sage. Gramps got me an autographed photo of Gene Autry when Autry visited Middletown one time.

I'd get in for free at the Strand also, and head for 'the booth' to watch movies from there. Great fun!

A few years later, after I had learned to play the Hammond organ, Gramps let me play the Strand's theater organ. Many years after that, I was given the opportunity to play a restored theater organ in Santa Barbara, CA. More about that later.

Theater Art

Back in the old days, movie theaters employed artists to make large posters that advertised coming attractions.

Gramps and Dad surprised me one Christmas with an electric train set. There were two trains - a new Lionel one with a 20-wheeler engine, and my old Marx train that I had played with when I was younger.

Gramps had the Paramount's theater artist landscape two large sheets of plywood with green 'grass' and 'roads' for toy cars and trucks.

Gramps surprised me again, years later, by having a theater artist make four wood fold-up music stands for me. They looked just like regular 'big band' music stands, and had a big letter 'R' on the front. The 'R' stood for

17

'Rhythmaires', my band in junior high and high school!

Little did I know that someday I'd meet another movie theater artist in California. My wife Holley Gene's dad, Eugene Hammond, was a theater artist in Riverside, CA before he started working for, and eventually becoming a manager for, Sears (Roebuck and Co.).

Junior High School

Roosevelt Jr. High was another few blocks (uphill) from Lincoln Elementary. I walked it every day. My remembrances of Roosevelt are as follows:

- In 7th grade, Geraldine Jones dug her fingernail into my right arm (ouch!) because I had been teasing her. I stayed away from Geraldine Jones. The mark she made on my arm never faded completely away.
- Wood shop (I loved to work with wood).
- Eighth grade math – taught by the football coach.
- The Von Trapp Family (their story was told in the movie "The Sound of Music") visited Middletown and performed in Roosevelt's auditorium.
- I played bass viol for several school musical plays. The orchestra leader was Miss Valda Wilkerson (a redhead). I would go on to play bass viol in the Middletown Civic Symphony under her direction.

Middletown Civic Symphony

Playing in the Middletown Civic Symphony was quite an experience. I was 13 years old. Performances were given in the High School's auditorium.

I played bass viol. See performance program to the right.

MIDDLETOWN CIVIC SYMPHONY ORCHESTRA

SOLOISTS
PHILIP D. DREIFUS, Violinist, and ERIK KAHLSON, Violist

SOLOIST
SOULIMA STRAVINSKY, Pianist

ORCHESTRA PERSONNEL

FIRST VIOLINS
†Mrs. E. H. McCandlish,
    Concert Mistress
†Mrs. H. H. Harrison
†Mrs. Forest Bowman
 Edward Mulloy
 Anne McGill
 John Adrion
 Mrs. Bert Blair
 John Root
 Don Gibson
*†Philip Dreifus
*Hobart Schoch

SECOND VIOLINS
†Mrs. H. D. Wren, Principal
 Miss Helen Weinberger
 Mrs. Fred Johnson
 Hale Dodds
 David Gaw
 Martha Ramsdell
 Rita Curry
 Carolyn Wagoner
 Beth Dieterly
 Marianne Davidson
 Trent Bobbitt
 Catherine Springer
*Herbert Silbersack

VIOLAS
 Bert Blair
 Dorothy Diver
 Ruth Roess
*Erik Kahlson
*Joseph Sherman

CELLOS
†H. H. Harrison
†Mrs. Gordon Carr
 Dorothy Davidson
 Mrs. William Giles
*Victor Rice

DOUBLE BASS
H. J. Aronoff
Mickey Leffler

FLUTES
Jane Wiley
Eleanor Shartle

PICCOLO
*Robert Cavally

OBOES
Edwin Bloedow
*Marcel Dandois

CLARINETS
Robert Bell
Bill Stiehl
Jim McGraw
*Emil Schmachtenberg

BASSOONS
*Hans Meuser
Robert Raker

HORNS
Joe Franklin
Mrs. Bruce Evans
Barbara Coffman

TRUMPETS
Gene Young
Jack McLaughlin
Ronnie Finkleman
Ross Finkelman

TROMBONES
Jerry Lapham
Fred Tyson

TUBA
Bert Sheard

BASS TROMBONE
Carol West

HARP
Mrs. Robert S. Sutton

TYMPANI
J. H. Waxweiler

PERCUSSION
Herschel Day
Fred Kruse
Gwen Stamper

LIBRARIANS
Carol West
David Gaw

* Member of the Cincinnati Symphony Orchestra.

† Member of the Middletown Civic Symphony Orchestra since its beginning in 1941.

19

Freddie Tyson, who I grew up with on Arlington Avenue, played trombone (you remember, Mrs. Tyson was my 'almost' first grade teacher). Barbara Coffman played French horn. Later in life, Barbara was killed in a car/train accident. I went to high school with them both.

I played bass viol next to Mr. Aronoff, who was very good. I went to school with his son, Mike, and his daughter, Marcia.

I could keep up with Mr. Aronoff on most musical selections, except for one – "Capriccio Italienne" by Tchaikovsky.

Beginning at measure 156, twelve measures of pure hell followed.

At this point in the music, we were to use a bow to play the strings (the notation from the composer to do this was 'arco').

The music for these twelve measures consisted of 32nd notes (very fast notes), all of which had to be played with a bow!!!

No, that's not enough exclamation marks. (!!!!)

Tchaikovsky — Capriccio Italienne, Op. 45

Kontrabaß

Tell you what, I'll use exclamation marks to represent the twenty-four 32nd notes to be played in each measure:

[(!!!!)(!!!!)(!!!!)(!!!!)(!!!!)(!!!!)]

And this was just one of the 12 measures that were going as fast (as my dad used to say), ". . . as a bat out of hell!"

Mr. Aronoff executed these notes flawlessly.

I sort of slid my fingers down the strings (because the notes were going up the scale), bowed like crazy, and hoped for the best. What I couldn't achieve musically, I tried to make up for by grimacing and by dressing up in my best clothes.

It was during my years at Roosevelt that I began to blossom a little. I had been taking piano lessons from an early age. Roosevelt's Principal, Andy Roper, allowed me to practice on the school auditorium's concert model Hammond organ during summer vacation. I practiced nearly every day. As a result:

- I got to play the "Star Spangled Banner" on Roosevelt's organ for all student assemblies.
- I began playing organ for the early Sunday service at St. Paul's Church. My piano teacher, Monna Conn, was the organist for the main service. I played every early Sunday service afterwards, all the rest of my school years.

The Rhythmaires

I started a dance band, 'The Rhythmaires'. One of our first 'gigs' was playing for a student dance held in Roosevelt's gym. The gym's piano was in terrible shape – out of tune, and some notes were not functional. I worked hard to tune the piano and to make it playable before the dance.

Some notes could be tuned. Others could not.

I do not admit to cutting out a few piano strings here and there with wire cutters to eliminate those that couldn't be tuned.

The Rhythmaires played for dances all around the area. We even made two appearances on Cincinnati (Ohio) TV.

I played piano when there was one, acoustic bass if not.

Tim Lamphier, Jim Clark, Spencer Duffey, Bill Brown
Back row: Dave Daubenmire, me, Curtiss Dunbar

As I grew older and entered high school, I began to help my dad more and more at the funeral home. We referred to it as 'The Place'.

I played the organ for funeral services. I delivered rental chairs to various events and locations (yep, that was a form of advertising), and helped out on ambulance trips and 'death calls'.

'Death calls' is self-explanatory. Ambulance trips - maybe not.

Back in those days, there were no paramedics, EMTs, or 911 responders. Funeral homes had one or maybe two vehicles for making ambulance trips (an ambulance and/or a 'combination' hearse/ambulance). Whenever the phone rang and an ambulance was needed for 'an emergency', Dad and I (or one of the other men at 'the place') would run to the garage (or jump out of bed, get dressed) and go get the ambulance to make the run.

The objective was to get the patient to the hospital emergency room as soon as possible.

I'd usually ride in the back of the ambulance with the patient. If the patient was severely hurt, Dad would ride in the back and I'd have to drive.

It snows in Middletown. I've had the doubtful pleasure of driving against traffic up the center of a two-lane, one-way street, going fast, in the snow, with the siren blaring!

I learned a lot about life – and death – working at 'The Place'.

Some of my worst experiences were the deaths of two of my friends from school. One of them, Kenny, played sax in my band, 'The Rhythmaires'. Kenny injured his leg and developed cancer. I picked him up at his home and took him to the hospital for the last time. I played his and his girl friend's favorite song, "Unchained Melody", at his funeral.

The other person, Barbara, was the daughter of a Middletown minister. She played French horn in the Civic Symphony. She was killed in a train/car collision.

I could not bring myself to view her lifeless body.

I was impressed by her father's composure during her funeral service. You just had to know he was strong in his faith, and that he knew his daughter was now in a better place.

Dr. Decker

Then there was Dr. Decker. Dr. Martin Decker was our family doctor. He saw me every week for years to give me injections for my allergies.

On one of my ambulance runs to the hospital, with a male heart attack patient, Dr. Decker happened to be in the Emergency Room.

Dr. Decker tried to revive the man, even with injections into the heart, but to no avail.

Dr. Decker broke into tears because he could not save his patient. I was impressed and will forever remember Dr. Decker for his sincerity.

Artificial Heart

Back to the funeral business.

While I was still in high school, my Dad had a friend named 'Doc' who sold embalming fluid and a pump to inject the fluid into the body. It was Doc's belief that if this pump could simulate the pumping of the human heart, the process could be improved. He wanted the pump to come up to speed from zero, then reduce the flow back down to zero or near zero, over and over again. He also wanted to be able to control the rate/strength of flow. He wanted, essentially, an artificial heart.

I told Dad I'd see if I could come up with something.

I looked through my past issues of *QST, Popular Electronics Magazine,* my *Allied Radio* catalog, and some electronic components I had lying around from past projects. I came up with an idea. I asked Dad to drive me to Dayton, Ohio to SREPCO (Standard Radio and Electronic Parts Company). SREPCO was the ham's 'Candy Store' in the greater Dayton area. I bought some parts and Dad drove me home.

A few days later, I had a working 'breadboard' (a model) to demonstrate. It consisted of some resistors, capacitors, a rectifier, a rotary selection switch, and a relay.

'Doc' took my breadboard with him and came back a month or so later – with a production model. It worked great!

'Ham' Radio

I loved my experiences with the 'ham' radio fraternity.

I had to learn Morse Code and be able to pass a code speed test of 5 words per minute. I passed the FCC (Federal Communication Commission) 'Novice Class' exam in Cincinnati, and got 'on the air' sending Morse code to anyone who could receive and acknowledge my transmissions.

My first receiver was a Hallicrafters Model S-40B. I made my first transmitter. It was a one-tube transmitter housed in a plastic refrigerator food container. It put out about 1 watt of power. Compare this to the average AM radio stations' output power of 1000 watts. 'Clear channel' AM radio stations operated with 50,000 watts.

A year or so later, I passed my 'General Class' FCC exam. The code speed test was 13 words per minute. There was also a technical part in the exam.

Dad took me back to SREPCO in Dayton and bought me a Johnson Viking VII transmitter and a Hammarlund HQ140-X receiver.

Now I was in business! I was transmitting with 180 watts and had a really good receiver. And, because I now had a General Class license, I was not limited to just Morse code. I could transmit and communicate with other 'hams' using voice!

I went on to put a shortwave receiver in my parents' car. I was able to receive (in Ohio) transmissions from Argentina!

In my last years at home, I taught Morse code classes. I could send and receive Morse code at speeds in excess of 20 words per minute in my head without writing anything down.

One never forgets Morse Code. We have a dove in our backyard in California that coos "dit-dah-dit". We call him our 'pirate bird' because that's Morse Code for 'R' (arghh!).

Dad erected two steel towers in our backyard and, with my help, several odd-looking antennas. One tower could be cranked up and down and held a directional antenna that could be rotated to 'point' to any direction on earth.

I talked to 'hams' all over the world and acknowledged contact with them by exchanging 'QSL' cards by mail. Hams used 'Q' codes when sending Morse code transmissions to save time. For example, 'QTH' means 'what is your location?' 'QSL' means 'can you acknowledge transmission?' I learned that QST (the magazine title that caught my eye years before) was the 'Q' code abbreviation for 'a transmission directed to all ham radio operators'.

Honor Society, Dean's List

While in high school, I was elected a member of the National Honor Society (based on scholastic achievement).

I was also selected to go to Ohio Boys' State, where we learned about state government.

I made the Dean's List in college.

First Computer

In high school, I read a scientific article about the binary number system. I was fascinated! I then learned that the new electronic computers being developed utilized the binary number system in their design and operation. I was hooked!

At the time (1956–1957), there were no personal computers. There were no 'Commodore 64' computers. The only computers around could only read information from punched paper cards, had electron tubes, and existed mostly at academic institutions.

I wanted to build a computer.

If I were successful, maybe I could win a college scholarship.

I figured I could use electro-mechanical parts (like pinball machine parts) to do the job.

I didn't have the knowledge to make an electronic computer (I was a junior in high school). Neither would I have been able to afford making one.

I spent hours in my basement putting things together. When I was done, my computer occupied several big sheets of plywood, and had about a mile of wire connecting things together. There was also a 'control panel' consisting of two rotary telephone dials and a bank of seven lights to read out the 'answer'.

The computer could multiply two numbers (up to 9 times 9) and display the answer in binary code. For example, 9 times 9 = 81. The answer would be displayed on the seven lights (from left to right) as

'on', 'off', 'on', off, 'off', 'off', 'on'.

These lights represented the binary number sequence 1010001, or, from right to left, '1' + '16' + '64'.

I visited 'Uncle' Marlin in Illinois. I was named after Marlin. He was Dad's cousin but I called him 'Uncle'.

Uncle Marlin introduced me to his friends in Chicago who were executives at Westinghouse and part of the national Westinghouse Science Talent Search committee.

The Westinghouse Science Talent Search, since 1942, has helped find and encourage talented high school seniors to pursue careers in science, math, engineering and medicine.

I don't think Uncle Marlin's friends believed what I had done (my computer). I received an Honorable Mention in their competition.

In Middletown, things were different. The American Rolling Mill Company (ARMCO), was the steel mill in my home town. ARMCO was known for inventing stainless steel. The president of ARMCO awarded me first place in their regional science competition and gave me a check for $2400! Big bucks back then!

I had been accepted at Princeton University, the Air Force Academy, the Naval Academy, MIT, Cornell University, and other schools. I chose to go to Cornell because three of my high school classmates chose to go there as well.

Cherry Cake

Mom made the BEST cherry cake!

It was a white cake with pieces of maraschino cherries and walnuts throughout. I loved it!

But then, after a while, and after having it 'all the time', I made the mistake of asking Mom to fix something else for dessert.

I shouldn't have done that. I must have hurt her feelings because she never fixed cherry cake after that.

She did fix it one more time for me, years later, after I begged her for some of her "delicious cherry cake"!

Thanks, Mom.

Grandpa and Grandma Leffler (William and Stella) lived on a farm on Kyles Station Road, near Middletown and Hamilton, Ohio.

They had an outhouse on the farm until the plumbing was installed. The last time I visited the farm, the outhouse still stood out back (unused), near their backyard 'victory garden'. Most everyone had a 'victory garden' in their backyard during WWII.

I remember going into the barn and playing with the corn husker (a machine you put ears of corn into). It 'shucked' the corn kernels and ejected the left-over bare corn cob.

The Lefflers raised chickens for food and for eggs. They'd drive over to Middletown once a week and bring us eggs. Grandpa Leffler drove a Model 'A' Ford. Grandma Leffler didn't drive (my maternal grandmother didn't either).

Dad, after a while, bought them a 'newer' car – an old four-door Dodge.

I remember visiting G&G Leffler at their farmhouse.

I would look through their collection of *National Geographic Magazine.*

Another thing that was fun was to pull out a 'pop gun' target game from a cabinet in their family room. I'd shoot a cork 'pop gun bullet' at little spin-around targets.

Grandma Leffler would fix a dish that seemed to be a family favorite. It was pieces of chicken suspended in a gelatin of some sort.

The other things I remember about visiting the farm:

- Pumping water from the farm's well in the front yard - you needed to 'prime' the well with water in order to bring water up from the well.

- One time Aunt Ruth held a chicken by its neck, and, with a quick shake, broke its neck. We had chicken for dinner at a family get-together that evening.

Here's a photo taken of the Leffler family members at that get-together.

1: me; 2: Uncle Howard Alden (Aunt Marjorie's husband); 3A: Mom; 3B: my unborn sister, Peggy; 4: Grandma Leffler; 5: Uncle Norman; 6: Grandpa Leffler; 7: Dad; 8: Uncle Leon (Aunt Ruth's husband): 9: Aunt Marjorie; 10: Gail (aunt Ruth's daughter); 11: Aunt Pearl (Uncle Norman's wife); 12: Aunt Ruth; 13: my sister Barbara; 14: Jack (Aunt Pearl's son from her first marriage).

The Leffler farmhouse still stands. I was able to take my family back there to see it. The present owners were gracious enough to let us walk through the house. During this last visit, I discovered in the basement that the beams that held the up house were made of hand-hewn timbers.

While I was there, I looked up at the tall trees swaying in the breeze, and was transported back to my childhood.

Marlin T. Leffler

My Dad's cousin, Dr. Marlin T. Leffler, worked for Abbott Laboratories where sodium pentothal was developed. An injectable general anesthetic, also known as 'truth serum,' sodium pentothal saved many lives in the field during WWII. Marlin grew up not far from the Leffler farmhouse.

Aunt Ruth

Dad's sister, Aunt Ruth, was the first person to make an injectable form of penicillin suitable for humans. Penicillin also saved many lives in WWII - and it saved my life when, as a child, I contracted osteomyelitis after crushing my finger in a car door.

Was this another synchronicity?

Aunt Marjorie

Aunt Marjorie, my dad's other sister, was an astrophysicist. She and her husband worked at the Palomar observatory, operated by Cal Tech, in the San Diego (CA) area.

Uncle Norman

Dad's brother, Uncle Norman, served our country in the Army during WWII. Afterwards, he was one of the best Mercedes Benz mechanics ever! Uncle Norman didn't need fancy instruments to tune up a car. He just looked at the car's radio antenna and tuned up the car so the antenna wouldn't vibrate when the engine was running.

Dad and Uncle Norman took me fishing once for little 'butter fish' (that's what my family called them) down on a creek near the Leffler farmhouse.

Uncle Clarence and Aunt Edna

Uncle Clarence and Aunt Edna had a dairy farm down the road a ways from Middletown. They were wonderful, loving people.

One time, Uncle Clarence took my dad, Gramps and me rabbit hunting on his farm.

We got some rabbits, and I learned about 'field dressing'. Do you want to know what this means? If not, *skip the following explanation!*

Field dressing meant:

- Step on the dead rabbit's head
- Grab the rabbit's rear legs and pull

The head would come off. Then, the hunter could 'gut' the body with a knife, leaving its 'innards' in the field.

(end of 'field dressing' explanation)

Once, as I was taking a bead on a rabbit with my .22 rifle, my dad stepped in front of me. I quit pulling the trigger just in time.

When Uncle Clarence died, his funeral was held in his farmhouse.

Not long afterwards, Dad received a 'death call' for Aunt Edna. I went with Dad to their farm. Aunt Edna had died sitting at the kitchen table, looking out the window. So sad.

Physics

I loved Physics.

Mr. McCandlish was my high school physics teacher. Mrs. McCandlish was the violin teacher in town.

When I was a junior in high school, I placed first in Physics in the state of Ohio.

I was 7th in biology the year before, but nobody seemed to care.

While studying Engineering in college, I served as a Physics lab Teaching Assistant.

As I've said later in this book, I also worked as an engineer for the Dept. of Physics at Michigan State University.

Color TV

Edwin Land, the inventor of the Polaroid Land Camera, published his theory of color vision in a 1959 issue of *Scientific American* magazine.

Land suggested that the brain needs only a two-color sample to 'see' a full color scene.

For example, assume one were to take two photographs of a full-color scene on black and white film.

One of these photographs would be taken through a red filter, the other photograph through a green filter.

Next, the two photographs would be developed to produce positive transparencies.

Then, the transparency taken through the red filter would be projected onto a screen through the red filter. The one taken through the green filter would be projected through the green filter.

The result was that the two projected images 'combined' on the screen and resulted in a full-color scene – browns, yellows, etc.!

Land demonstrated that the same results could also be achieved by using two yellow filters differing in color by only a few angstroms of wavelength.

Why am I telling you all this?

After reading Land's article, I got the idea that such a concept could be used to convert the many black and white TVs existing at the time into full color TVs. RCA's 3-color TVs were just coming into being in 1959.

I wrote a paper explaining my basic idea.

I phoned RCA headquarters at the Radio City Center in New York City.

An RCA vice-president took my phone call, and after I had explained my concept to him, invited me to come to New York.

I met with RCA executives who decided to send me to RCA's research labs at Princeton, NJ. Before I left their presence, I heard one of them ask another, "Do you think such a concept could work?" The other executive answered, "This reminds me of the time when a young Vladimir Zworykin presented his ideas to us. We need to at least look at his (my) ideas." (note to the reader: Zworykin, the 'father of television', invented the iconoscope – the first TV camera - and the kinescope, which reproduced the TV images on a picture tube.)

At RCA's Princeton Labs, I was met by John Mitchell, who had developed RCA's three-color TV system. I explained my idea for a two-color system that could convert existing B&W TVs to color.

Mitchell understood my concept. He then told me that RCA had tried a two-color system, but the results were less than desirable. Colors appeared washed out. RCA felt they just couldn't achieve satisfactory levels of color saturation with a two-color approach.

I will never forget and will always appreciate the open-mindedness of these men – enough so to listen to a 20-year-old's ideas.

ARMCO

Halfway through college, I came home to Middletown to make some money.

The major employer in my hometown was a steel mill, the American Rolling Mill Company (ARMCO for short).

ARMCO invented stainless steel, and made other custom batches of steel in their open-hearth furnaces. They hot-rolled and cold-rolled steel in various forms and shapes for their customers.

ARMCO also produced steel products like corrugated, galvanized irrigation drainage pipes.

I worked for ARMCO as a 'fill-in' employee for a while - if someone were ill, I'd go do his job. For example, I worked in the drainage pipe department once. Later on, I went to work in the open-hearth furnace part of ARMCO where they made the steel 'batches'.

One time, I was assigned to go help the 'steel plate' department.

You know the steel plates they put down on streets that are being worked on? Those steel plates were being made by a department in ARMCO.

When I arrived for my shift, there was this tall stack of heavy steel plates – and a conveyer belt.

My job was to take a pair of tongs, grab a steel plate from the top of the stack, and throw it down onto the conveyer belt.

I put on my heavy gloves, picked up the tongs, grasped the top sheet in the stack, and attempted to pull it down onto the conveyor belt.

Can you envision me holding onto the tongs, my feet nearly off the ground, trying to move this immovable object?

I tried. Lord knows, I tried.

I told my supervisor, "I don't think I can do this job."

My supervisor said, "Don't worry. 'Tiny' Tyndall will be here to help you."

'Tiny' Tyndall appeared. My God, he was big!

Tiny put on a pair of gloves, took a pair of tongs, and grasped the top steel plate in the stack.

WHAM!

Tiny pulled the top sheet off the stack onto the conveyor belt.

For the rest of the work shift, I 'helped' Tiny.

(More exclamation marks - !!!).

Choir Director

I needed some income while attending engineering college in Indiana. My young wife, Becky, (we married 9/5/59) worked as a waitress on the Indiana Turnpike. I had a part-time job working in a precision gauge manufacturing company.

I learned that the First Christian Church in town was looking for a choir director. I applied and got the job.

Every week, I dutifully hand-transcribed the SATB choir music (Soprano, Alto, Tenor, Bass) for the next Sunday's service. I also held a weekly practice with the choir so they could learn the music I had transcribed.

I thought I was doing well, but a month or so later, I was 'let go'.

Oh well, on to bigger and better things.

Michigan State Cyclotron

While I attended Graduate School at MSU, I worked for

the Department of Physics, helping them with the initial development of their Sector-Focused Cyclotron (SFC). Here are some of the parts I helped with.

- Peltier Junction Thermoelectric Cooler – the magnetic field inside the cyclotron had to be measured accurately. A new magnetic field sensor (the Hall Effect transducer) had recently been developed. It was the magnetic sensor of choice at the time, but it had one drawback. The transducer needed to be maintained at a constant temperature. I designed a temperature controller utilizing a solid state Peltier Junction. The Hall Effect transducer was mounted on the Peltier Junction and its temperature was held constant within plus and minus 0.1 degrees Fahrenheit.

- High Voltage Probe capable of measuring several thousand volts

- Low Wattage Exciter for the cyclotron cavity – coincidently, MSU had picked a 'ham' radio transmitter to excite the cyclotron cavity at HF radio frequencies. It was the same 'ham' radio transmitter that I had used at home when I was a boy! I knew how to operate it instantly. Another coincidence?

- Before I left MSU, I designed a one-million-watt radio frequency amplifier to excite the final design cyclotron cavity. To put a perspective on this – the most powerful AM radio stations in America operate at 50,000 watts. Voice of America was allowed to operate at 1.25 million watts.

As Paul Harvey used to say on the radio, "Now, here's the rest of the story."

Today's gold standard for finding cancer cells in the human body is the Positron Emission Tomography scan, or PET scan.

An irradiated sugar solution is injected into the patient and the patient is placed in the PET scanner. Cancer cells love sugar, so they 'light up' during the scan. Three members of my family have had PET scans – including myself.

Just another technological achievement?

A Michigan State University newsletter reported: "Nuclear irradiating agents created by a cyclotron at MSU are used in medical procedures such as PET scans."

Is this a synchronicity?

Another 'coincidence':

The MSU cyclotron was designed to operate at HF high (radio) frequencies – the same band of frequencies I used as a 'ham' radio operator in my earlier years!

Was I supposed to be a 'ham' so that, someday, I could help people get well by contributing to the design of the MSU cyclotron???

You tell me!

I think so.

Stan Kenton Jazz Workshop

In 1959, Stan Kenton held his first Jazz Camp at Indiana University. Student musicians from all over the country gathered to attend Kenton's workshops on performance, improvisation, and arranging. As Kenton would say, the students took a "bath in jazz".

In the early 60s, a camp was opened at Michigan State University.

I heard that Stan Kenton was to conduct a jazz workshop one evening at MSU. I went to listen.

After the workshop, several of the Kenton band members

retired to a local restaurant and played some impromptu jazz. There was a piano there, so I joined in. What fun!

Becky

Becky, my wife of 28 years, gave me three wonderful children – Christopher, Heather, and Nicolle – for whom I am eternally grateful.

We were married in Middletown, Ohio, before I left to attend college.

Becky had two friends worthy of note.

- One of them used to date Elvis Presley.
- The other appeared as a 'Playboy Bunny' hopeful on Hugh Hefner's 1959 B&W TV show out of Chicago.

Becky eventually became a cardiac care nurse. I know she's saved and helped save many lives.

I remember one time, Becky and I took our kids to Hawaii. We stayed at the Sheraton Rainbow Hotel on Waikiki.

As we walked along, a baby near us started choking on something. Becky went over and extracted an object from the baby's throat. The baby was OK. We walked away as the parents comforted their child.

Later that day, Becky answered a knock on our hotel room door. The baby's father had tracked us down.

He rushed into the room and gave her a grateful hug!

Becky's mom and dad, Viola and Bill Frisby, were wonderful people. Vi could make the BEST cornbread. Bill headed up the cold-rolling mill at ARMCO. What I remember most about him is that he used to say, "and et-cet-ree" (instead of 'etcetera').

BTW ("by the way" for all you texting illiterate folks - like

40

me), my 96 yr-old Aunt Pearl in Missouri (Uncle Norman's wife) likes to say "on that" all the time. Example: "So that's all that's new on that."

Honeywell

I was offered several engineering jobs after leaving college. I chose to go to work for Honeywell Military Products Group in St. Petersburg, Florida. One of the reasons was that Grandma and Grandpa Francis wintered in Clearwater Beach, not far away.

My first day on the job, I was asked to translate a schematic diagram of a new logic module assembly into a pictorial wiring diagram that could be used by production line personnel to produce the assembly.

Honeywell had been trying to find someone to do this job for a while.

That first day on the job, I stayed and worked all night.

In the morning, I presented my supervisor with a completed wiring layout of the assembly.

They were impressed.

After that, I was given several other 'tough' jobs, but I was able to do them all. Maybe because I could think out of the box – and I liked challenges.

Bomber Pilot Jacket

One of these 'tough jobs' was to troubleshoot an airborne computer suspected of having problems caused by cold temperatures.

I put on a WWII Bomber Pilot jacket and crawled into a temperature chamber with the computer and an oscilloscope - and found the problem. Brrr!

41

Boogie

Boogie (our dog in Florida) was a beagle.

I'd watch him lie motionless in our backyard until a bird would swoop down on him, trying to attack him.

He'd then jump up and catch the bird. Surprise!

In Florida, we lived in an area which had only recently been reclaimed from swampland.

One day, my wife Becky saw an alligator in our backyard, running back and forth along our fence, trying to find his way out. Becky called the sheriff.

Two young officers showed up. One of them was shirtless and had a rope belt. He took off his belt, tied up the alligator, put it in the trunk of the sheriff's car, and took off.

A few weeks later, I found the body of Boogie in a nearby swampland. He'd encountered another 'gator'.

Electrostatic Gyro

Honeywell developed a very advanced navigation system in the late 60s. The primary sensor consisted of a metal sphere, electrostatically-suspended in an evacuated spherical metal cavity. Once suspended, the sphere was then electrically spun up to 30,000 rpm! Photoelectric sensors kept track of the spinning mass and its orientation relative to the metal cavity. The metal cavity in its frame was fastened to the vehicle (aircraft, submarine, etc.). As the vehicle moved, a computer would calculate speed and direction. Knowing the initial position of the vehicle, present position could be calculated by the computer.

The ESG system was extremely accurate, making it applicable for missions requiring precise navigation. The system was chosen for the F-117 Stealth Aircraft.

The system also maintains its accuracy over long periods of time, making it especially suitable for long-term-submerged nuclear submarines.

The ESG was initially flight-tested at Wright-Patterson AFB in Ohio. Testing was being hampered by an unexplained problem. Occasionally and randomly, the system would 'go to sleep' for approximately 21 minutes, then come back to life.

I got sent to Ohio.

I surmised that something in the computer was causing its program to go down the wrong path until some counting mechanism in the code counted up to or down to a certain number. At that time, the program would recover and get back on its correct path.

I examined the code in the computer program and found one unused location that, with a little imagination, could become a counter. There was enough 'room' in this 'counter' to count for 21 minutes and a few additional seconds.

I forced the computer program to go down this 'counting' path – and the 21 minute problem manifested itself!

But what could cause the computer to jump out of its normal routine and start 'counting'?

I eventually found that a randomly-occurring, momentary failure of an electronic component was the culprit.

Its failure would dump a large number into the 'counter' and start the process. I was able to observe this failure with an oscilloscope.

The offending component was replaced and the '21 minute problem' was no more.

I was granted a Top Secret clearance in 1967. I've qualified for its renewal ever since.

Access to a SCIF is limited to those with special security clearances and a need-to-know. All activity and conversation inside a SCIF is restricted from public disclosure.

SCIFs are constructed to foil any attempts of electronic surveillance from the outside. A SCIF can be a room enclosed in a tightly-sealed metal shield, known as a Faraday cage, and utilizing methods of jamming to secure (from the outside) internal conversations and the sounds produced by operation of the equipment within the facility.

A SCIF can also be a mobile configuration that can be deployed using air, ground or maritime resources.

Sensitive Compartmented Information is only briefed, discussed, and stored in an accredited SCIF. Programs and operations under the SCI paradigm are usually not publicly acknowledged by the U.S. government.

There are SCIFs in the U. S. Capitol in which members of Congress are routinely briefed on intelligence, counterintelligence and military operations. Components of the U.S. Department of Homeland Security such as the Office of Intelligence and Analysis have SCIFs. Many U.S. military installations in the United States and around the world are equipped with SCIFs.

The last SCIF I've worked in is at a military installation in California. To get to my desk and into my computer, here are the levels of security that I must go through:

- Vehicle ID at the military installation's front guard gate

- Personal ID at the front gate

- Entry code on external door to the SCIF

- Entry code on the door to my office area within the SCIF

- Combination to my Mosler safe drawer – to gain access to my computer's removable hard drive

- Install the hard drive into my computer and enter my username and password

Security personnel are present throughout the SCIF. They actively ensure that all activities within the SCIF are in compliance with program security requirements. All personnel working within the SCIF are required to take periodic refresher training in these requirements.

All paper and electronic media are cataloged and their security level defined. All are then stored within the SCIF and routinely inventoried by Document Control personnel.

Computer passwords must be changed on a regular basis. Entry door codes are changed when SCIF personnel are reassigned.

Background music is played on wall-mounted speakers. This is done so that if someone on the outside aims a laser beam at an exterior wall in an attempt to 'hear' internal conversations, they'll hear the background music instead. However, there are no restrictions on what kind of music can be played. Randomly, I get to hear my own recorded music which I donated to 'the cause'.

Other SCIFs in my life:

- Area 51 is the legendary Top Secret facility in the Nevada desert. Every building is a SCIF. No one knows what's going on in those SCIFs except the people who work inside them. Perimeters are patrolled by guard dogs and armed officers. More about Area 51 later.

- Lockheed 'Skunk Works' in Burbank, California (now closed). SCIFs were everywhere!

- Northrop Aircraft in Newbury Park, California (now closed). As Manager of Advanced Design and R&D, I was responsible for project personnel working in an off-site SCIF. Even though I had a Top Secret clearance, I couldn't know what the project was, and I wasn't allowed in the SCIF. As their manager, I had to turn in annual performance evaluations for these personnel. To do so, the Vice President of Engineering told me what to write. He was cleared on the program. I was not.

There were two other SCIFs at Northrop that I knew about. I worked in one of them, called 'the Cone of Silence'. It reminded me of the old TV program "Get Smart" starring Don Adams as bumbling secret agent Maxwell Smart. The 'Cone' had a hidden entrance, and was constructed of ¼ inch thick, welded-together, steel plates on all six surfaces (four walls, ceiling and floor). It was big and held many combination-locked file cabinets and work cubicles. There were alarmed 'man traps' on all the ventilation ducts.

One of the most unusual SCIFs I've been in is the one for the DIA (Defense Investigative Agency) at Wright Patterson AFB in Ohio. Entry/exit is through 'bank vault' doors. For more, see 'Algerian Nuns' later in this book.

Area 51

I moved my family (wife Becky, son Christopher and daughter Heather) to Thousand Oaks, California in 1967 so I could work at Area 51. My family could not know where I was from Monday through Friday. They were given a 'clean' emergency phone number, however, in case my family needed me.

Back then, no one could even know the term 'Area 51'.

Lockheed made available two old Lockheed Constellation aircraft (a model 'G' and a model 'H') at Burbank Airport to transport personnel back and forth between southern California and Area 51 in Nevada. We affectionately referred to the Constellations as 'Connies'.

It's interesting to note that, years later, my wife Holley Gene and I have two close friends named 'Connie'.

Area 51

My first job at the 'Area' was Flight Test Operations - planning and debriefing.

The Lockheed A-12 Blackbird was being developed and flight tested at the Area.

The A-12 was capable of Mach 3 flight. Its turn radius (at 3,300 feet per second) was about 80 nautical miles!

After takeoff, the 'Blackbird' had to be refueled before beginning its mission. It took all that fuel just to get it airborne.

I remember that one of the test flights took the 'Blackbird' to the East Coast of the U.S. and back. No ground radar even detected that it was up there!

SCDM

The job of the Signal Conditioner and Data Monitor was to record the A-12's position and other parameters such as roll, pitch, angular rate, etc., on magnetic tape.

In operational use (photographing hostile locations), this information would aid mission analysts in their assessments.

There was so much electrical noise on all the aircraft's signal and power lines that the electronic logic modules in the SCDM would get 'clobbered' and randomly set themselves to incorrect states. The noise would sometimes cause the SCDM to record a data scan that hadn't been requested by the payload - and even this data was unreadable.

My solution - whenever the SCDM got a request from the payload to take a scan, we'd clear the states of all the logic modules, take the scan, and record the data on tape. My thinking was that there would be very little time for a noise pulse to come along and 'upset the apple cart'.

I called it the Clear and Scan Mod. It worked great!

By the way, 'upset the apple cart' reminds me of the A-12 project's code name – 'Oxcart'.

Colonel Hugh Slater, Commander of the Oxcart program, sent me a letter of appreciation.

DEPARTMENT OF THE AIR FORCE

1129TH USAF SPECIAL ACTIVITIES SQUADRON (HQ COMD USAF)
POST OFFICE BOX 88
BOLLING AIR FORCE BASE DC   20332

SUBJECT: Letter of Appreciation   24 July 1968

TO   Mr. Mick Leffler

1. It is a sincere pleasure to express my appreciation for the truly commendable contribution you have made to the successful accomplishment of our detachment mission. Your individual dedication, knowledge and exemplary ability assisted immeasurably in the development and overall final success on a revolutionary project of highest national interest. Additionally, you have shared in the outstanding praise frequently received from highest government levels and the recently presented Air Force Outstanding Unit Award.

2. Having worked with you through periods of frustration and success has been the highlight of my Air Force career. Without your individual loyalty and devotion to duty the superior results and status now enjoyed would have been impossible. All have reflected the highest credit upon you, the detachment and the United States of America.

3. Again my gratitude and the best of luck in the future.

Sincerely

HUGH C. SLATER, Colonel, USAF
Commander

After a year at Area 51, I was promoted and assigned to another SCIF, this time in southern California. There was important developmental work on a Mach 3 hypersonic drone going on there.

The D-21B drone's mission was to overfly hostile territory and take reconnaissance photos. It was to be the next generation 'Blackbird,' but this time with no pilot on board.

An earlier incident, with Francis Gary Powers being shot down in his U-2 reconnaissance aircraft, prompted this development. (I used to park in Powers' parking space at Lockheed after he had left the program).

The D-21B was intended for reconnaissance missions deep into enemy airspace. It carried a high-resolution camera over a preprogrammed path, then released the camera module into the air for retrieval, after which the drone would self-destruct.

It was initially designed to be launched from the back of a 'Blackbird' variant. After a fatal accident because of a flawed launch, the D-21B was modified to be launched (dropped) from a B-52 Stratofortress.

The B-52 mother ship could carry a D-21B under each wing. The mother ship's navigation system utilized an automated star tracker which continually updated the mother ship's position.

Data links from the mother ship to each of the two D-21Bs kept the drones' navigation systems up to date. At the time of launch, the B-52 would 'drop' the D-21B. Seconds later, the drone's rocket booster would fire and power it up to its operational speed (Mach 3) and altitude (80,000 feet) - at which time the drone's propulsion system would take over.

I remember two exceptional events.

The first: I was called to Beale AFB in northern California to support an 'operational generation' (not a test flight).

The day of the mission, I sat in the command center with the Air Force colonel in charge of the operation. The mission was to be supported by several tanker aircraft positioned around the globe to refuel the B-52 during carryout. Some of these tankers had already been deployed.

We got a call from the flight line that a 'red light' had been received during systems run-up.

I hopped into a Jeep and was driven out to the B-52.

I was asked to make a 'go/no-go' decision for the mission.

I told them, "No-go."

It broke my heart to call everything off – but I knew we had no reason good enough to put all those personnel at risk if the integrity of the system had been compromised.

Later testing revealed that the 'red light' circuitry was susceptible to noise. We fixed that!

The second exceptional event was another operational launch.

I had a Top Secret clearance, but still was not allowed to know what the mission was.

I asked them to give me access so I could run a simulation of the intended route to ensure all would be OK with our navigation system.

The answer was, "No."

The mission was unsuccessful. The D-21B failed to follow the planned route.

After the fact, I was allowed to run a simulation of the mission in the lab.

I found that the direction cosines (the navigation equations used to define the drone's position) had a 'singularity'. That is, the equations couldn't handle one of the positions the D-21B had to fly over on this particular mission.

I wish they had let me run the simulation before the mission.

Back Home

I wanted my three kids (daughter Nicolle was born in California) to experience a few things about growing food and raising animals.

I planted artichokes on our big back slope. Put in some tomatoes, too.

I built two cages that were up off the ground along the backyard fence. We got two rabbits to go in the cages.

I built an aviary in the backyard alongside the house. We got some partridges and finches for the aviary.

I also built a chicken coop in the backyard. We got some hatchling Rhode Island Red chicks at a local feed store. We kept them in an incubator in our garage until they were big enough to live outside in the chicken coop.

I hoped that the chickens would lay eggs, so my kids could experience getting the eggs and maybe even selling them to our friends and neighbors. But the chickens weren't laying eggs.

I went back to the feed store. That's when I learned I needed a couple of roosters!

We had all kinds of eggs after that!

We also raised Mallard ducks. They lived in the backyard. We had a drake and a hen – and eventually little chicks that followed their mother all around the yard.

Duck eggs taste good!

At the time, we lived on <u>Drake</u> Drive in Thousand Oaks. Get it?

We got some Bantam chickens, too, but they didn't want to live in the chicken coop – so they lived in and ran around the backyard. Occasionally, one or more would fly over the backyard fence. We wouldn't see them for a day or so – but they'd always come back.

[An interesting sideline: Later in my life, I met my second wife, Holley Gene. Her grandfather, years earlier, had raised and sold Bantam chickens to Hearst Castle, William Randolph Hearst's mansion in California.]

─┤ Background Measurement Satellite ├─

In the early 70s, the U.S. wanted to develop the capability of detecting a hostile ballistic missile launch.

The concept was to put a satellite into orbit that would continually map the background radiation of the earth's 'limb' (where the curvature of the earth meets the blackness of space).

The satellite would contain a multi-spectral set of

cryogenically-cooled infrared sensors that would continually map and keep track of - in the satellite's computer - what the 'normal' earth's infrared background was.

In the event of a ballistic missile launch, the 'normal' earth's radiation background would change. This would produce a warning that an exceptional radiation event had occurred.

I designed the satellite computer but have never heard whether the project went forward.

Lockheed L-1011 Aircraft

I left Honeywell and went to work for Frank Wright and 'Rollie' Samuelson (both ex-Honeywell men) at Lockheed in Burbank, California. They were in charge of developing the avionics (aviation electronics) for Lockheed's new L-1011 jumbo passenger jet.

The Lockheed L-1011 was, in my opinion, the most advanced commercial passenger aircraft of its time.

I was a Design Specialist for its avionic systems. The L-1011 had the:

- 1st Category 3A (all-weather blind landing) Auto-land system (automatic landing system)
- 1st Area Navigation System
- 1st Flight Management System (FMS)
- 1st 4 dimensional FMS

Category 3A Autoland – This system was capable of landing the aircraft automatically and safely even though the crew could not see the ground. I spent a year in England working with British Airways and the CAA (the British Civil Aviation Authority) proofing and certifying this system. I examined data from every automatic CAT 3 landing performed by every L-1011 aircraft in the British Aircraft fleet - and I analyzed and followed up on any and all anomalies.

The system was certified down to CAT 3A standards - which means if the Captain still can't see the ground at 12 feet radar altitude, the captain must call for a 'go-around'.

The truth of the matter is, if the crew can't see the ground at 12 feet, the aircraft will probably be on the ground by the time the Captain gives the command, "Go around," and the 1st Officer and the aircraft respond.

So, in effect, the L-1011 system was capable of a Cat 3C landing. Cat 3B weather means "can't see the ground until you're on it." Cat 3C weather means "can't see the ground even when you're on it".

They wanted a new navigation system for the L-1011, and my navigation skills fit right in.

In 1971, the L-1011's Area Navigation system was the first of its kind. It had three (3!) inertial navigation system platforms, two navigation computers, two control panels with electronic displays, and an electronic map system that displayed aircraft current position, as well as the intended flight path for the flight.

I was Lockheed's Principal Development Engineer for this world's first area navigation system. Several companies contributed to its development:

- The software by Decca in England.
- The inertial navigation systems by Collins in Cedar Rapids, Iowa.
- The computer and systems integration by ARMA on Long Island.
- The EACS (Electronic Automatic Chart System) by Astronautics Corporation of Milwaukee.

The first Area Nav system was certified with an initial 'A' version software. The 'B' version was capable of storing all the flight routes and airport data in the U.S. airspace on one magnetic tape cassette!

Is Donny There?

Rolls-Royce (UK) built a new engine, the RB-211, for the Lockheed L-1011. The RB-211 was one of the first 'high bypass' designs, with an enormous front fan and a thrust of 40,000 pounds. This design broke new ground, but its development proved to be very costly. Early in 1971, RR went into bankruptcy.

Lockheed's chairman, Dan Haughton, rescued Rolls-Royce by arranging for the U.S. Congress to guarantee a new loan of $250 million. This gave Rolls-Royce the money it needed. The firm emerged from bankruptcy and turned the RB-211 into a successful engine.

I got sent to England, along with a Lockheed vice president named 'Archie Smith' (not his real name).

Our assignment was to make RR 'toe the line', and to ensure that Rolls was doing its best to make the RB-211 a good product.

Archie could get quite outspoken if he thought things weren't going as they should. Archie was a difficult person to like, however, we got along just fine. An angry Lockheed employee allegedly threw Archie off a roof once (!)

Archie and I identified that RR had a problem with the design of the RB-211's oil cooler.

We 'held their feet to the fire'. We told them we'd be back in two months to see what progress they've made on improving the design.

We came back in two months.

RR had prepared a nice presentation about everything except what had been done (if anything) to improve the oil cooler.

I 'became' an Archie Smith.

"We gave you an assignment to fix things with the oil cooler – and you have shown us nothing you've done to do so in the last two months!"

I could see Archie smiling at me out of the corner of my eye.

RR eventually fixed their problem.

What does this have to do with Donny Osmond?

Here's what happened.

On my visits to meet with Rolls Royce, I stayed at what used to be a nunnery.

During my first visit, it happened that the Osmonds were touring England.

It also happened that the Osmonds' manager had the last name of 'Leffler'.

All the teenage girls that were fans called hotels and other places in the area, trying to find out where the Osmonds were staying.

I got a phone call in my room one afternoon. "Is Donny there?"

The rest of my stay there, my socks were washed, carefully folded and placed on my made-up bed.

Luton, England

I was sent to Luton, England to support Court Line Airlines in their initial use of the Lockheed L-1011 Area Navigation System.

57

I was in Court Line's cafeteria when I overheard a conversation between two Court Line L-1011 pilots.

One said he'd noticed on a recent flight that his Horizontal Situation Indicator (HSI) veered off course momentarily. Then, a few moments later, the copilot's HSI did as well.

After my experience with the D-21B equations 'blowing up' at certain positions on the globe, I called the U.S. company back home that made the navigation systems Court Line was using.

They confirmed that there was a computational 'singularity' at the position on the earth where the pilot had observed the anomaly.

Flying over the North Pole

The S3A Viking aircraft was designed for use by the U.S. Navy to identify and track enemy submarines. The Viking also provided electronic warfare and surface surveillance capabilities to the carrier battle group.

I was asked to evaluate the S3's navigation system.

Because of my previous experiences with singularities on the earth, I asked the system to fly due north to the North Pole, which is located at 90 degrees north latitude. That's the highest latitude on earth. As you fly over the North Pole and go down the other side of the earth, latitude should start to decrease.

As I 'flew' the system up a longitude line to the North Pole, the latitude readout was 89 degrees, 89 degrees thirty minutes, 90 degrees, then 90 degrees and some more minutes – an impossibility.

Needless to say, they fixed that.

Dissimilar Functional Redundancy

It was clear to me by now, after experiencing the singularities in the D-21B, S-3A and Court Line navigation systems' software - it's a false hope to have redundant, even triply redundant systems, if they're all of the same design. A latent defect in the design could manifest itself and bring everything down.

A case in point – back on one of the early Apollo missions, a triply redundant system began to exhibit multiple failures. The mission did not fail – but it was only because one of the three systems was of a completely different design. The one system that was different from the other two kept on working.

My conclusion: utilize what I call 'dissimilar functional redundancy' in order to have true redundancy in a design!

British Airways Assignment

I got sent to England to help certify the British Airways L-1011s for 'blind weather' automatic landings.

My family came to England with me.

I leased a house in Pinkneys Green, a suburb of Maidenhead, England - a short commute from London's Heathrow Airport where I had an office.

Pinkneys Green was a nice area. The house had four bedrooms upstairs, and a separate garage. There were two schools just over the backyard fence. Chris, Heather, and Nicolle attended these two schools – no bus or train rides, like many English school children had to endure.

I bought a ten year old VW camper bus from an American mother. She and her children were leaving the Heathrow Airport's Holiday Inn to catch a plane for home. She sold it to me in the parking lot for $350!

I bought an old piano for four English pounds (about $10 at the time). My girls, Heather and Nicolle, took piano lessons at our house.

I found a similar good deal on a used color TV and console radio/phonograph. I also bought an American washer and dryer (considerably bigger than their English counterparts) from a U.S. Air Force family living at a nearby air base. The washer and dryer were designed for the U.S. electricity standard, but ran OK on the English electric standard. The motors got a little warm, however.

I also bought another used English car to drive back and forth to work.

One time, coming home from work, I saw four English women standing next to their 'dead' car in the snow. They were freezing and nobody was stopping to help them.

I stopped. "Can I give you ladies a ride somewhere?"

One of them looked at the others and said, "Don't you know it would be an American that would offer to help us."

My girls, Heather and Nicolle, took English horseback riding lessons.

My son, Chris, joined the Scout troop at Pinkneys Green. That's where Baden Powell founded scouting back in the early 1900s. Chris and I would give the boys a ride in our VW camper. A camper bus full of boy scouts - what fun!

I had been an Assistant Scoutmaster at our home in California before going to England.

The scoutmaster of the Pinkneys Green troop also taught wrestling. Chris wanted to learn to wrestle, so I took him twice a week for lessons.

Several months later, Chris began wrestling for England at the Jr. Olympic level. I took him to wrestling meets around England and Wales. We usually stayed the night in pubs that offered overnight lodging at very reasonable rates – especially for boys representing England in championship events.

Chris loved Elton John's music – "Benny and the Jets", etc. Elton John lived in nearby Windsor.

Chris slept overnight several times on islands in the Thames River with his new-found English boy friends.

One afternoon, as my family walked along the Thames River in Maidenhead, Nicolle pushed Chris into the water because he was teasing her.

Ice Water Feeling

At the end of my year's assignment with British Airways, and before returning home to the U.S., I took my family throughout Europe for a month. We drove and camped overnight in our Volkswagen camper bus.

One sunny afternoon in Monaco, I had just walked out of a bank after changing some money.

Suddenly, it felt like someone had poured ice water over my head! I also had a feeling of dread.

I knew this was a sign that something was terribly wrong.

I wanted to phone home to America, but Becky, my wife at the time, talked me out of it.

Two weeks later, upon returning to my office at Heathrow Airport in London, one of my co-workers told me that my father had passed away two weeks earlier. It was at the same time I had experienced the 'ice water' feeling!

My dad had been riding an old-fashioned bicycle (big wheel, little wheel) in a parade – and had collapsed and died suddenly.

BTW (by the way), my dad died on my second wife Holley Gene's birthday in 1977 – ten years before I met her. More about Holley Gene later.

Coincidence? (!!!!)

Blondie

At one time, I owned several rental homes in Thousand Oaks, CA. I did all the lawn maintenance on my rentals. My tenants didn't know I was the landlord. They thought I was just the landscape guy. That way, I could keep my eye on what was going on.

One of the rentals was a nice three bedroom ranch home that had an orchard and a horse stable. I built the stable to house "Dream", the horse I bought for my girls Heather and Nicolle after we returned from living in England for a year. The stable could hold two horses - for Dream, and for my girls' friend's horse. It even included space for a goat. The goat was a companion to the horses and kept them calm.

I listed the property for rent.

One day, when I was working in the yard, a car drove up and several guys got out.

They said they were interested in renting the house, and would it be OK to look around?

They liked the house and gave me first and last month's rent in cash(!)

I said OK, but wondered what I was getting into.

Later on that afternoon (I was still working at the house), a big black limousine pulled up in front and a pretty blonde stepped out.

It sure looked like 'Blondie' (Deborah Harry) – a famous rock star at the time!

The Lockheed L-1011 aircraft had an amazing system called the Flight Management System (FMS).

When I was on assignment in England to certify the Autoland system, I flew around Europe with Capt. Hugh Dibley, Chief L-1011 pilot of British Airways.

The purpose of the trip was to capture (on magnetic tape) flight data resulting from Capt. Dibley's operation of the L-1011.

We flew out on the British Airways 'line' for several days. Dibley flew the aircraft in an optimum manner on all segments.

At the end of the trip, I sent the mag tape recordings back to Lockheed in California. Lockheed used this information to develop the Flight Management System (FMS) – a system well ahead of its time.

Another story about Capt. Dibley.

One evening, I met Hugh for dinner at the Proud Bird Restaurant, located at the end of one of the runways at LAX airport. The restaurant was pretty much empty except for the two of us – and a group of somber-looking people sitting over in a corner.

Curiosity got the better of us. We walked over to the group and asked what was wrong.

It turned out they were members of the Human Resources department of Rockwell International.

They had just finished laying off workers associated with the recently-cancelled B-1 bomber program.

Hugh and I bought them all a drink, and left.

When I returned to the states after my British Airways CAT 3 assignment, I went to work helping develop the FMS.

The FMS could fly the aircraft, using the least amount of fuel for the flight of the day, at a speed that was the most economical for the flight's assigned altitude, weight of the aircraft (passengers, luggage, fuel, etc.), and weather conditions encountered in flight - pretty good, huh!

The FMS was given national recognition by the Museum of Science and Industry in Chicago. This was the same year the clip-on-a-finger blood gas monitor was honored. I was privileged to attend the ceremony along with others from the FMS development team.

Four-Dimensional Guidance

One of the problems of flying is that, even if you've flown the aircraft in its most economical manner, once you arrive at the destination airport, you might have to fly in a holding pattern, waiting your turn to land.

Wouldn't it be better to be assigned an arrival time and fly in such a manner that you will arrive at the destination airport at that time? No more wasted fuel!

That's exactly what the 4D FMS was able to accomplish – arrival time control, with time being the 4th dimension of aircraft guidance.

I proposed a concept of doing so. Lockheed went ahead with implementing my suggestions.

I remember standing in the cockpit of the flight test L-1011 during the first test of the 4D FMS. Our arrival time accuracy was within four seconds!

Additional demonstration flights were made into Dallas/ Ft. Worth. I presented technical papers at several FAA Air Route Traffic Control Centers (ARTCCs). Lockheed even produced a movie about the 4D FMS. A young 'me' was featured in it.

Other efforts I contributed to in Lockheed Advanced Design:

- The first all-color electronic flight instrument displays. These were featured on the front cover of Aviation Week magazine. Gulfstream Aircraft in Savannah, Georgia, contacted me for permission to use my design ideas in their new Gulfstream V aircraft.

- I co-authored with Boeing and Douglas Aircraft team members, and under FAA sponsorship, four volumes of design guidelines for developing advanced aircraft systems, including such items as:

  o Voice recognition interface

  o Time critical displays (including synthetic voice presentations)

  During our research, an oculometer was used to track flight crew member eyeball activity to determine crew response times, what they were looking at, and for how long.

- We tested the effectiveness of various types of voice presentations – for example, the Captain's mother's voice, a hysterical female voice, etc. Also, should the voice present the situation at hand, or, if the situation were time-critical, give a command to follow? The final Collision Avoidance System employed a stern male voice command, "Pull up! Pull up!"

- We developed the first Cockpit Display of Traffic Information (CDTI) system. This display showed nearby aircraft in flight and displayed them in red if safe separation distances were not being maintained.

- I proposed a windowless flight station for a DARPA space plane. Views of the outside environment and all flight displays were electronic. The high temperatures encountered at Mach 5 speeds prohibited the use of windows.

Algerian Nuns

A crowd of about 500 Iranian students seized the American embassy in Tehran on Nov. 4, 1979. Of the approximately 90 people inside the embassy, 52 were held captive until the end of the crisis. In an attempt to free the hostages, President Carter applied economic pressure and several diplomatic initiatives.

Carter's failure to resolve the crisis contributed to Ronald Reagan's election in 1980.

After Reagan's election, and with the assistance of Algerian intermediaries, successful negotiations began. On Jan. 20, 1981, the day of President Reagan's inauguration, the United States released almost $8 billion in frozen Iranian assets and the hostages were freed - after 444 days of detention.

President Reagan wanted to do something to thank the Algerians for their efforts in getting the American embassy hostages released.

The Algerian Air Force at the time was operating Russian-built MIG-21 supersonic jet fighters. The avionics of the MIGs were aging and needed to be upgraded to improve the aircraft's mission capabilities.

I got sent to Algeria.

Before I could go, I was summoned to Wright-Patterson AFB in Ohio. The Defense Investigative Agency (DIA), in residence there, wanted to brief me on some things they wanted me to look for.

The DIA at WPAFB operates in a large SCIF whose doors are reminiscent of those of a large bank vault.

This was at the time when the latest Russian fighter was the MIG-29 (NATO designation: 'Fulcrum'). The DIA was interested in knowing if any Fulcrums were in operation in Algeria. They were also interested in knowing about certain features of the MIG-21s that might have already been upgraded.

I left for Algeria with 'Ken' - another engineer (not his real name). We were being sent as representatives of a southern California division of Lockheed Aircraft.

Upon our arrival, 'Ken' and I were met by two Algerian nuns dressed in brown and white habits. They said they were nuns. They looked like nuns. They said they were there to help with any language translation that might be necessary.

The four of us climbed into a Jeep, and the nuns drove us out to an airbase in the Algerian desert.

We were met there by an Algerian Air Force officer and escorted to a hangar housing a single MIG-21. He spoke perfect English. Why did we need the 'nuns'?

Ken and I went to work crawling around the aircraft, looking at things like the radar, communications gear, and the instruments in the pilot's panel.

The wiring behind the panel was quite worn and needed to be replaced.

I discovered an interesting operational feature of the Algerian MIG-21. The pilot and his aircraft could be sent off on a mission with the pilot not knowing where he was going. That information would be relayed to him later in the flight.

We saw no MIG-29 Fulcrum aircraft. However, our entry into and exit from the airbase was direct and without any meandering about. The 'nuns' were very efficient about that.

We went back to Lockheed and put together a proposal for updating the Algerian MIGs. A few weeks later, a Lockheed vice president invited me to go back to Algiers with him and his team to present the proposal to the Algerian Ministry of Defense.

No nuns were there this time.

Seattle Proposal Assignment

I had flown to Atlanta to present a paper on 4D flight to Delta Air Lines.

The night before my presentation, I received a phone call in my hotel room.

Lockheed's Vice President Dan Tellep wanted representatives from each of Lockheed's divisions to attend a meeting in Sunnyvale, CA the next morning. I had been chosen to represent the Burbank, CA division.

I never made the presentation in Atlanta.

Tellep wanted to go after a big business opportunity being offered by the FAA (Federal Aviation Administration).

The FAA wanted to upgrade all air traffic control centers and towers in the U.S. – that is, for the entire national airspace! Tellep wanted attendees to decide which Lockheed division should team up with Boeing, form a new venture company alliance, and put together a major proposal effort.

A lot of hands went into the air. I reminded everyone there that Lockheed's Burbank division was the only one producing a commercial passenger aircraft. Also that we had been working with the FAA on air traffic control projects for several years.

I was selected to fly to Seattle the next day and begin planning an approach with Boeing, our major competitor for years, but now our new partner.

Lockheed and Boeing formed a new venture company named NASCO - which stood for National Airspace Company.

I spent the next 6 months working in Kent, Washington (near Seattle) on the proposal effort. It was kind of like my old Area 51 days. I would fly out of Burbank every Monday and back to Burbank every Friday. I flew Alaska Airlines. At the time, Alaska would give you a free 'Princess' telephone every time you'd fly with them. I had a pile of new Princess phones at home to give away at Christmas!

I was selected to be the Technical Work Director for the project. Boeing did not like the first man offered for the job. They didn't think he was 'aircraft savvy' enough. I was introduced as the next candidate.

A Boeing vice president took me to a hangar where a single aircraft resided. It was a Boeing 'Jenny' biplane from WWI – and it had been immaculately restored. I teared up. They picked me for the job.

----------------------------| Suit Coats: |----------------------------

We wanted photos of everyone on the NASCO team to appear in the proposal. Not everyone had a coat and necktie with him. So those of us who did, 'lent' them to our fellow team members for the photos. We had no clothespins or masking tape. Guys would hide behind the person being photographed and 'grab' or 'pull on' the coat to make it 'fit' better. Everyone looked good in his photograph.

One of the features of our proposal was that we guaranteed to the FAA that NASCO would deliver trained specialists (100 of them total) to air traffic facilities around the country on the day after contract award (!!!).

I was chosen to define the curriculum and set up training classes for these 100 individuals.

NASCO had retained two ex-FAA Regional Directors as consultants on the proposal. I worked with them in defining what courses should be taught, as well as the courses' content.

NASCO even went so far as to fly some of us and our wives back to the Washington D.C. area to pick out homes, in case NASCO was awarded the contract. NASCO headquarters would be located near 1600 Pennsylvania Ave. (the White House address). Our residences would be located in Reston, VA – a beautiful nearby community.

NASCO didn't win the competition because (as I was later told) our Boeing partner over-priced the bid.

We had two ex-FAA executives on our team. And they had a good idea of how much money the FAA had in their budget for this work. Apparently, their recommendations fell on deaf ears.

Holley Gene

In 1987, I found myself separated from Becky and living alone. I was uncertain about what to do with my life. I turned to music to fill my time.

I met my second wife, Holley Gene, in 1987. She had raised her two daughters, Carrie and Wendy, by herself. Carrie now has five living children. Wendy has three. Both are examples of what good parenting can accomplish – no matter what hardships come along.

Holley Gene is an 'intuitive', and is musically talented. She taught music and organ for many years.

My life with Holley Gene has been one of spiritual awakening and learning more of God's plan for all of us.

Holley Gene has authored four books:

- *Letters To My Friends*
- *Re-creating Vintage Clothing* (she's also a costumer for turn-of-the-century and Biblical clothing)
- *In Remembrance of You* – an account of her grandfather's automobile trip across the U.S. in 1903 – and of her re-creation of his trip in 1985 (in a 1902 car!).
- *Enlightenment – We are all meant to be enlightened.*

and a musical chord book *Quick Keyboard Picture Chords*.

We have played organ (she) and piano (me) for several churches and for many rest homes and benefit events. We have also recorded our music and that of promising young artists we've come to know.

Holley Gene has helped me put together five books of sacred music:

- *The Sacred Medley Book*
- *Angel Music*
- *Christmas Medleys*
- *God's Offering*
- *In Jesus' Name*

and a sixth book, *Love Music*.

All of our books are available on Amazon.com

The Mayflower and William Penn

Holley Gene's ancestors came to America on the Mayflower. William Penn, an ancestor of Holley Gene's dad, gave a land grant to an ancestor of my father.

How's that for a coincidence?

In 1987, I purchased an electronic grand piano, a synthesizer keyboard, and a sound module. All of these had been designed to be compatible with the new MIDI (Musical Instrument Digital Interface) standard. These digital keyboards and the sound module were connected to a computer (a Commodore 64 at the time). All of the musical 'instruments' could be 'played' on the musical keyboards and these musical 'events' recorded by the computer.

For example I could 'play' a trumpet sound residing in the sound module by playing the keys on my musical keyboard. The computer would remember the trumpet part that I had just played. I could then repeat the process with another sound, e.g., violins, and then layer the violin part onto the trumpet part. In this manner, I could put together an entire 'orchestra'.

I had to remember the particulars of each instrument. For example, a clarinet can play only one note at a time. A guitar is strummed, so I would have to 'strum' the keys on my keyboard. Playing a 'harp' on my keyboard was the most fun.

Putting the music together in the computer was pleasing to me because it brought together my two worlds – technical and musical.

I started buying music and making my own arrangements.

There was no place in my town that had a good selection of printed music. I found one in nearby Ventura, CA.

A lady named Holley Gene ran Music Alley, a printed music concession inside a music store there. (It wasn't until much later that I realized 'Music Alley' was a play on words – for 'musically').

Holley Gene would order music for me that was a little

more challenging than the average. She would also pick out music that she thought would interest me.

One day, Holley Gene told me that her father had been admitted to a local hospital for heart surgery. I knew he enjoyed music from the 30s and 40s.

I made a cassette tape of some of the music I had been playing at home and brought it to Holley Gene to take to her dad. She told me he enjoyed listening to it.

Holley Gene phoned me one day and said that the community musical theater in Ventura was looking for a Musical Director – and would I like to apply?

I did apply in person. The musical they wanted to perform was "L'il Abner".

I told them about my MIDI equipment and let them hear some of the music I had done. I got the job.

After my interview, and as I was leaving Ventura for home in Thousand Oaks, I was rear-ended by a car traveling at high speed. The collision spun my car around and totaled it. I went to the hospital but was released with just minor bruises, aches and pains.

Holley Gene offered that I could stay at her place that evening. And that the next day, I could borrow her car to do what I had to do concerning the accident (file an insurance claim, etc.).

Holley Gene is interested in numerology, and on a previous visit with her, she 'did my numbers' and told me my number was "3".

The day after the accident, I got into her car and put the key into the ignition. I looked down at the mileage displayed on the odometer.

The mileage was 33,333.3 miles!

Coincidence – or synchronicity?

73

Back to "L'il Abner".

From just the piano music part, I put together orchestral arrangements for all the songs in the musical. (I could 'hear' the orchestrations in my head).

My intent was to take my digital 'orchestra' and play the songs 'live' at every performance. I tried to store all the songs in my Commodore 64 computer, but there was not enough computer memory to do so.

Then I saw an announcement that a new computer, the Atari 1024, had just become available. The Atari had more than 10 times the memory of my Commodore 64.

I purchased the Atari and 'played' my digital arrangements from the Commodore 64 into it. My 'orchestra' could now play 'live' at every performance.

A software company named Sonus had written the MIDI software for the Commodore. I contacted them and told them about "L'il Abner".

Sonus told me only one other such digital musical had been performed in the country – somewhere back in Connecticut. "L'il Abner" would be the first all-MIDI musical ever to be given on the West Coast!

Some of the Sonus folks even came to Ventura to see the performance.

─────────────┤ **New Zealand Visits** ├─────────────

I had visited New Zealand twice. The RNZAF wanted to upgrade their A-4 Skyhawk aircraft.

I was sent to their airbase at Ohakea on the North Island to talk with RNZAF officials about their requirements – and to inspect a nearby deserted crop-dusting aircraft factory to see if the upgrades could be performed there.

I liked New Zealand.

Holley Gene's daughter had married a 'Kiwi' (a New Zealander) and she and her family were living in New Plymouth on the North Island. I visited New Zealand several times with Holley Gene.

Another strange story (or a 'synchronicity?') was my first visit to New Zealand with Holley Gene.

Holley Gene wanted to visit her daughter Carrie, to be there after the birth of Carrie's second child. She asked me to go along.

We planned the trip in order to be there about two weeks after the birth.

On the day of our departure from California, I bought a Ventura newspaper from a street vending machine at the airport bus stop.

The date printed on the front page of the paper was October 7th – incorrect because it was actually the 5th. Every other page in the paper had the correct date on it - October 5th!

This certainly caught my attention – and what are the odds that I would even have noticed this in the first place?!

Was this some kind of omen? We wondered if we should even go on this trip.

But we did go.

When we arrived at New Plymouth, Holley Gene's daughter met us at the airport, stomach 'out to here'. No baby yet.

Later that day, she went to the hospital to have the baby. Sadly, the baby was born dead!

It had taken Holley Gene and me 26 hours, door to door, to make the trip. And, because we had crossed the International Date Line, the date was October 7th

– the date misprinted on the front page of the Ventura newspaper!

(!!!!) (!!!!) (!!!!) (!!!!) (!!!!) (!!!!) (!!!!) (!!!!)

On another one of our visits, I learned that the community theater in New Plymouth was in final rehearsal and planned to put on a musical during our visit. They needed two more songs for the musical right away.

A medical doctor, and a friend of Carrie's, had a recording studio and some MIDI gear at his home.

I arranged and recorded the two songs they needed for the musical. As a 'thank you', we were invited to the opening night performance a week later.

The Missing Book

On another visit to New Zealand, Holley Gene purchased a single book from a set of books titled *Mysteries of the Unknown*. The store did not have any of the other books in the set.

Upon our return to California, we went to a local 'swap meet'. There sitting on a vendor's table were all the other books in the set. The vendor apologized that she didn't have the complete set. The title she was missing was the title we had purchased in New Zealand.

Was this a coincidence or a synchronicity? What's the difference between the two?

Here's what I think a coincidence is. Let's say two card players are each holding a deck of cards. Each then draws a card from his deck. If they both draw the same card, the three of hearts, that's a coincidence – the occurrence has no 'message' or 'meaning' to either card player. On the first draw of a shuffled deck, each card player has a 1 in 52 chance of drawing the three of hearts.

A synchronicity would be that the two card players drew the same card seven times in a row – and that the seven card numbers were player #1's telephone number, and were player #2's telephone number backwards! A few days later, each card player remembered a similar experience occurring with a distant relative of his family.

Was the '7 card' experience telling the card players they might be related? There's a message in a synchronicity.

Submarine-launched Drone

In 1987, I was hired by Northrop Aircraft to be their Manager of Advanced Design and R&D.

One of the worrisome threats at the time was the enemy's capability of being able to launch an ICBM from a mobile launch platform. This meant that their ICBMs could be moved at any time, even hidden in forests, making it difficult to find and counter the threat.

One solution was to design a submarine-launched missile that would carry several drones. The missile would release the drones which would then 'glide/parachute' to their operational altitudes. The drones would employ multi-spectral sensors (infrared, ultraviolet, even acoustic) to locate and neutralize the enemy's mobile launchers.

The drone's infrared sensors would detect any heat signatures. The ultraviolet sensors could see through foliage. The acoustic detection system would first produce acoustic 'pings' that would strike the ICBM or launcher's metallic surfaces and be reflected back as a signal to the drone.

Some of Northrop's best engineers worked on defining this advanced concept.

To my knowledge, the concept was never developed.

My boss, Ron (once Chief Engineer on the Space Station), and I both left Northrop Aircraft after becoming disenchanted with higher management. The aerospace industry went through some hard times in the period 1987 – 1991. I found myself out of work for most of that time.

An ex-boss of mine from Lockheed contacted me and asked if I'd like to work with him again. This time, we would both be consultants on a large proposal effort.

The U.S. Navy's fleet of P-3 patrol aircraft was aging and needed to be updated. In addition, each aircraft had various problems that also needed to be corrected.

The proposal effort started out in California, but it was later decided that the proposal team should relocate to an airfield in South Carolina where the actual work would be done.

The proposal team occupied a mobile structure located near the airfield's runway.

One stormy summer afternoon, a 'microburst' (a small 'twister') pummeled the airfield. It scattered several small aircraft around the field and 'weather-vaned' two jumbo jets that were parked nearby. Also, there was a P-3 aircraft fuselage (with no wings) up on jacks on one of the taxiways. The storm lifted the fuselage off the jacks and rolled it down the field like a rolling pin. The twister missed our mobile structure – thank goodness!

There was one thing I did on the proposal that I was especially proud of. It was expected that each P-3 aircraft coming in for repair and upgrade, would have different needs.

The costs of the repairs and upgrades needed to be estimated so that an overall cost of the proposed program could be given to the Navy.

Working with technicians who were familiar with the P-3

aircraft, I put together a list of all anticipated repairs. Next, I listed the minimum and maximum amount of work the technicians had estimated for each of these repairs.

I then constructed a Monte Carlo simulation using Microsoft Excel software. As each 'aircraft' (in my simulation) came in for upgrade/repair, each repair item was allowed to be either selected or not selected. The amount of repair work required for that 'simulated' aircraft was allowed to vary, in a random manner, between the minimum and maximum amount of work expected.

I ran 10,000 'aircraft' through the simulation to give the team a better understanding of the size of the overall project and the amount of time that might be required to repair/update all the Navy's P-3s.

Now, in those days, the pages of a proposal were usually hung on the wall – and 'problem' pages were printed on colored paper to give a better real-time idea of the proposal's status at a glance.

One day, we ran out of colored paper. I went to a local store and bought a ream of colored paper for $4.

When I returned to the proposal team site, the Proposal Manager got angry at me for buying the paper and told me not to submit my $4 purchase as an expense. He even followed me when I later went into the men's room and continued to yell at me there.

The end result of his anger was that I was 'let go' a few days later and sent back to California (!?).

Proposal Manager

After being out of work for two more years, another California aerospace firm hired me to be their Proposal Manager. I won three out of five major new business proposals for them in my first year on the job.

The biggest of the three I won was to replace all the ground acquisition radars in the United Kingdom (yes, even on the Falkland Islands). This 'win' was worth several hundred million dollars to my employer.

For this, I was given a 40 cents/hr. raise.

I quit the next day!

Travels with Holley Gene

Beside several trips to New Zealand, Holley Gene and I have been blessed to be able to see other parts of the world that have always been special to us.

Mexico

Puerto Vallarta – we honeymooned there in 1989.

One thing I particularly remember is walking down the street at 'siesta time' one day. All the stores were closed.

We passed a dress shop, and, there in the window was a beautiful, white satin dress. I wanted to get it for Holley Gene.

We found a street-side café and enjoyed probably the best ceviche we ever had there. We've been on a quest for better ceviche ever since, but we have found nothing else quite as good, yet.

When 'siesta time' was over, we walked back to the dress shop, which was now open.

We entered and asked if anyone was there (to help us).

A lady came out from the back room, and – I almost had a heart attack! The lady looked exactly like my dear departed Grandma Francis!!!

Was this another synchronicity?

We bought the dress and had a wonderful evening at Bogart's Restaurant. Everything was in white – Holley Gene's new dress, my clothes and shoes, the white draped fabric above our table – they even had a white piano (which I played).

Well, everything wasn't white. Holley Gene had red shoes on. The restaurant brought her a red pillow to rest her feet on. And they put a beautiful long-stemmed red rose on her plate before dinner.

Our hotel (Hotel Krystal) had a swim-up bar in the pool area. They served what (I swear) was a bacon-flavored tequila! We've been on a quest for bacon-flavored tequila ever since but have never found anything quite like it. I did find a sage-infused tequila in a restaurant in Ventura that was quite good, however.

Another of the things I remember about 'PV' was that outside our room, in a grassy park-like area on the hotel grounds, a lady was making 'sopes' for the hotel guests.

Holley Gene and I returned to PV for our 20th wedding anniversary. The same lady was still working at the Hotel Krystal!

Europe:

- Italy
    - Assisi – we visited St. Francis' church - a holy place. There were banners hanging in the church that said "Peace" in every language.
    - Florence – had our portraits sketched by an artist outside the Uffizi Museum
    - Rome – saw the Roman ruins and the Vatican

- o Padua – saw the Giotto frescoes

- o Sienna – saw the black and white tiled church that Galileo attended. We also visited the town square. It seemed to be a special place because all the young people congregated there to sing and dance.

- Paris
  - o Saw all the 'good stuff'
    - Eiffel Tower
    - Notre Dame Cathedral
    - The Louvre – with famous paintings by Rembrandt, Vermeer, and others. Sculptures like Samothrace (Winged Victory).
    - Place de la Concord and the famous water lily paintings by Monet.
  - o Saw the Sacre Coeur cathedral. Like the town square in Sienna, Italy, it also seemed to be a special place because a lot of young people congregated outside.

- Monaco – had a restful visit there.
  - o Took a boat tour around the beautiful harbor
  - o Saw the Palace where Princess Grace had lived.
  - o Re-visited the street where I had the 'Ice Water Experience' in 1977.

- Amsterdam
  - o Visited the Rijksmuseum museum to see paintings by Van Gogh and 'Night Watch' by Rembrandt.

o   Took a boat ride on the canals.

- Vienna

    o   Stayed at a hotel where Chopin had stayed.

    o   Visited St. Stephen's Cathedral.

    o   Had lunch at a restaurant by the Danube River.

- Salzburg

    o   Toured the castle

    o   Stayed in a guest house near where the Von Trapp Family lived (at least in the movie). Arnold Schwarzenegger stayed in the same guest house whenever he visited Austria.

- Heidelberg

    o   Visited the Church of the Holy Spirit. On weekdays the church is surrounded by little street vendor shops. To us, the church appeared to be a mother hen protecting her brood.

    o   Visited the castle.

- Turkey - an important part of early Christianity.

    o   Ephesus - Paul lived in Ephesus organizing missionary activity. He wrote his letter 1 Corinthians from Ephesus. It is thought that the Gospel of John was written in Ephesus, c 90–100 AD.

    o   Istanbul - the blue Mosque

- Greece

    o   Athens – We visited the Parthenon. We later dined in our hotel's rooftop restaurant, and had a lovely nighttime view of the Parthenon all lit up. It was beautiful!

- o Delphi – The Oracles of Delphi were women mediums to whom it was believed the god Apollo spoke. The Oracle would enter an enclosed chamber in the basement of the temple on Mt. Parnassus to receive her prophecy. She was most likely exposed to concentrations of a narcotic gas (like ethylene), strong enough to induce a trance-like state described as a floating euphoria.

  o Corinth - Paul chose Corinth as headquarters for his mission to the west. Luke's account of Paul's stay in Corinth is found in Acts 18:1-18.

- The Greek Isles
  o Patmos – The Cave of the Apocalypse where the Apostle John received revelations from God by means of a voice from a cleft in the rock and wrote the Book of Revelation. John was exiled from Ephesus, a short boat ride from Patmos around 95 AD.

  o Santorini – in my opinion, the most beautiful of the Greek Isles! The town is built on the top ridge of a huge submerged volcano's caldera.

  Holley Gene and I had an informal lunch with our cruise ship's captain. We gave him a CD of some of our music.

  On our departure from Santorini (at sunset), we got an invitation from the captain to join him on the bridge for the event. The view was breathtaking. Thanks, Capt!

- Spain
  o Flamenco dancing – the music and the rhythms.

- Gaudi's Church of the Sacred Family – still under construction (since 1882).

- Granada – I took a CD of my arrangement of "Granada" with us. Our tour guide played it for everyone there.

- Montserrat - a mountain top monastery in Catalonia, Spain.

- Israel

  - Jerusalem

  - The Sea of Galilee

  - Tabcha – I had written a song, "My Cup Runneth Over" (in my *Angel Music* book) about Jesus' feeding of the multitudes. There's a church erected over the location (a rock) where Jesus stood. I was overwhelmed.

  - Bethlehem and the Shepherds' Fields – are in the Palestinian Territory. In order to enter the PT, our Israeli Jew bus tour guide had to be replaced by a Palestinian tour guide. Then our tour bus was allowed to enter.

- Egypt – we visited Cairo, saw its museum, and then the Pyramids and the Sphinx in Giza. It was so hot in Giza, we decided to return to the air-conditioned tour bus and just look at the pyramids.

  - River Nile boat – We cruised the Nile River on a riverboat, like a small cruise ship.

    Here's another synchronicity for you.

    When we were shown to our cruise ship for the first time, we noticed its name, "Norma", the name of our son-in-law Christopher's mother. Holley Gene and I had taken Norma and her husband Bill to Sedona years earlier. They were a lovely couple.

Before we left to go to Egypt, we had heard from Christopher that his mother was quite ill.

When we saw the name of our riverboat, we knew in our hearts that Norma had made her transition.

- Hawaii – I had owned a condo in Kihei, Maui, years before I met Holley Gene. Also, Holley Gene's daughter Carrie and family lived near Hilo on the 'Big Island' of Hawaii. We made several trips there – the most memorable to:
    o Oahu – we visited the parents of Holley Gene's girlfriend and schoolmate in Bogota, Colombia.

    o Waimea, Hana, and Lahaina, on Maui.

    o Hawaii – Volcanoes National Park

- The Caribbean – Holley Gene and I took a cruise to the Caribbean. What happened there was another synchronicity. That's another story. See "The Pearl Story" later in this book.

Mick's Important (?) Conclusions

- All trees will look like cell phone trees someday. Cell phone trees never get cut down - and real trees know this.

86

- Once we figure out how to live forever, we'll no longer need to have sex. OMG! (if you're not of the texting generation, OMG means 'Oh, my gosh'). Don't feel bad. I only know OMG and BTW (by the way).

Adjunct Protocol

The horrors of 9/11 might have been prevented if certain pieces of information had been collected, analyzed, and a flag raised to alert the authorities. Consider the following:

- July 10, 2001: Phoenix FBI field agent sends memo to FBI Headquarters suspecting terrorists training in US flight schools.

- August 16, 2001: Zacarias Moussaoui arrested in Minneapolis by INS (Immigration and Naturalization Service – now - after 2003 - ICE, Immigration and Customs Enforcement). He was turned in by a suspicious flight instructor.

- August 22, 2001: French Intelligence tells the FBI that Moussaoui is not allowed to enter France - has ties with radical Islamic groups.

- August 23-27, 2001: Minnesota FBI agents write that Moussaoui might "fly something into the World Trade Center."

- FBI Headquarters unable to connect Phoenix, Minnesota, French reports.

It's obvious that we needed a way of putting together:

Massaoui + terrorist + radical Islamic +
flight instructor + World Trade Center

from data obtained across agencies and across differing security levels.

A system does exist that can examine various databases having differing levels of security without 'cross-pollinating' or compromising the sources. I consult for the company that developed this system, although I was not involved in its development.

Even if all the 9/11 information had been in the same database, a manually-directed search couldn't have put all this together.

Who would have known to search the database with the keywords listed above?

The adjunct protocol I conceived employs a content-directed search, i.e., one based on the actual data in the various databases.

The system would automatically and continuously search for instances of commonality (of names, events, locations, phrases, etc.) from different sources (e.g., ICE, FBI, CIA, etc.) and from reports at different levels of security (e.g., unclassified, confidential, secret, top secret).

With such a system in place, the Phoenix FBI field agent's report would have been immediately available for automatic and continuous search. The system would also have notified the agent that his report had been included in the database.

Also immediately available and included in the automatic and continuous search:

- The report from the INS in Minneapolis about suspicious flight instruction and Moussaoui's arrest.
- FBI entry of the French intelligence report that Moussaoui has ties with radical Islamic groups.
- The Minnesota FBI agents' report that Moussaoui might "fly something into the World Trade Center".

With 'Moussaoui' as an instance of commonality, the new system would make the connection:

Massaoui + terrorist + radical Islamic +
flight instructor + World Trade Center

and notify the proper authorities as well as those submitting the original reports.

I set up a website in 2007 (www.AdjunctProtocol.com) and sent e-mails to all the intelligence agencies I could think of, as well as to several 'think tank' organizations.

The website featured a working demo of my concept.

I never heard back from any of them – I really didn't expect to.

I took the website off the Internet after Osama bin Laden was tracked down in 2011.

It's interesting to note that a TV series, "A Person Of Interest", débuted in September, 2011. The series talks about a system that can put together information from several sources to identify people who will most probably be involved in serious situations.

Coincidence?

Backyard Wedding

Holley Gene and I attended a party at a friend's house one afternoon. We noticed one of the interior walls had been faux-painted. It was beautiful. We asked who painted the wall.

Long story short, we now have some faux-painted walls in our lovely home.

We have since become friends with the young woman artist – her name is Aryna. We took her to Sedona, AZ, one time so she could see the beautiful red rock formations there.

Guess what? We have a 20-ft.-long wall in our home that looks just like the water-stained red rock canyon walls in Sedona.

Aryna wanted to marry a nice young man from Texas. We accommodated them by having their wedding in our backyard. Fifty or so attended the wedding and the reception afterwards. Rev. Dr. Phil McKinley of the Santa Paula First Christian Church officiated.

Time and the Big Bang

At the mall the other day, I overheard a little girl say, "We'll see Daddy when he gets here." This sentence demonstrates everything my concept of time and space is about. "We'll see Daddy" (we will see Daddy) connotes a time in the future. 'See' is what she will do at that time. 'Daddy' is who she'll see at that time.

Later the same day, while we were at a restaurant for lunch, my wife exclaimed, "The last time we were here, we sat over there." Her sentence demonstrates how we use our notion of time and space to express our thinking.

If there were no time, we wouldn't have to conjugate verbs - there would be no need for a past, present, or future tense. Without space, there would be no room for a 'he', 'she', or 'it'.

We needed a Universe – that's why we had 'The Big Bang'. The Universe has to be big so there'll be enough room for everything.

Having pet an elephant once, why do it again? Just think about doing it with your imagination. The imagined experience won't be a lesser one. And think of all the time and trouble (and gasoline) you'll save moving through space and time to get to a real elephant.

The elephant may not be in our time and space, but it is in our mind, our being. It's the same with those who are no longer in our time and space. They are in our timeless realm. We can 'go' to 'be' with them 'anytime' we want.

Al, a friend of ours from church always used to say, "Gooooooooood morning! Life is good! And wonderful things are happening!"

Wherever Al is now, hopefully it will be a place that actually has a morning, so he can continue to make his famous exclamation. I thought to myself that 'out there' in the fabulous infinity of everything, there has to be an

INFINITE number of places with a 'morning' for Al to continue on in.

Einstein said, "Time is relative."

Did he mean: time is on a sliding scale?

Einstein's equation is E=mc2. If you rearrange his equation so as to define mass (m), you get m=E/c2.

'c' is the speed of light (186,000 miles per second). You must have 'time' to calculate 'speed' (miles per second). If time is 'singular' (cannot be defined), and therefore the speed of light can't be defined, mass can't be defined either.

If mass can't be defined, we need no space to put mass in.

When time can be defined, then mass can be defined, and we need space to put things in.

Since we needed space (to contain mass), we needed the Big Bang to create this space. The energy in the 'Big Bang' event came from the 'E' in E=mc2. When time and mass became defined (non-singular), so did energy.

The Big Bang occurred because and when time slipped out of its singularity into relativity.

In 1999 a theory proposed that our Universe is actually a thin shell (a mathematical synonym for 'brane').

A later theory (the ekpyrotic theory) hypothesized that the origin of our universe occurred when two parallel branes collided. The ekpyrotic model maintains that our universe did not start in a singularity, but came about from the collision of two branes.

Such a model supports my 'Big Bang' supposition.

Let's say one of two colliding branes (our primordial universe) did not contain the dimension of time, but the second brane did.

The second brane's collision with 'our' brane imparted its

time dimension, and the 'Big Bang' occurred.

Our Wedding

Talking about time makes me think of Holley Gene's and my wedding in 1989.

'Time' was the theme of our ceremony. In fact, my wedding ring is engraved on the inside with "Love Is Eternal", and there is no wedding date.

I had arranged and recorded all the music for the wedding – so that I (and my music) could be there.

Holley Gene and I and our attendants (our five children) were all dressed in turn-of-the-century fashions.

Here's a photo of Holley Gene and me in her parents' 1903 Oldsmobile taken just after we were married in her folks' backyard.

Holley Gene's paternal grandfather was one of the first to drive across the U.S. in 1903 – no roads, no gas stations. The route taken was west to east - from San Francisco to New York City, then on up to Portland, Maine.

Holley Gene's grandfather is looking down in this photo.

Holley Gene re-created the trip in 1985 in a 1902 Curved Dash Oldsmobile!!! She tells the story of both trips in her book *In Remembrance Of You.*

Here are a couple of synchronicities about the 1903 Curved Dash Olds.

When I was in high school in Ohio, long before I came to California and met Holley Gene, my dad purchased a full-size replica car of the 1903 CDO! He used it to advertise the funeral home and drove it in parades.

Is this just a coincidence?

Here's another one.

Later on, after Holley Gene and I were together, we decided to take a trip to Sedona, Arizona. Sedona is known for its scenic beauty and red rocks.

Never having been there before, I searched the Internet to see what might be an interesting place to stay. We decided on a place called "Sky Ranch Motel".

We flew from Burbank, CA to Phoenix, AZ, rented a car, and drove about two hours to Sedona.

As we approached the motel, we were astonished to see a 1903 CDO parked out front!!!

The motel was on top of a mesa and had a view of the entire Sedona area – beautiful red rocks, canyons, etc.

Also on top of the mesa was a Masonic temple. Holley Gene's dad, my dad – in fact, most all the men in my family had been Masons!!

Were these synchronicities telling Holley Gene and me that we were supposed to be together?

Holley Gene and her dad in his 1903 CDO

Another Sedona Story

A few years later, we took our pastor Phil and his wife Tana to Sedona with us. They were impressed with Sedona's beauty, as we had been on our first trip.

While we were there, we heard reports that there had been flooding in Atlanta, Georgia. Phil and Tana's daughter Lori lived in Atlanta.

Phil called his daughter's cell phone right away. When she answered, he asked, "How's your house?"

She answered, "OK, I guess."

"What do you mean – I guess?"

Lori said, "We're not in Atlanta right now."

"Where are you?"

"We're in Sedona, in Arizona."

!!!!

Of course, we were all awestruck.

We had lunch together - Phil, Tana, Lori and her family, and Holley Gene and me.

Coincidence? No, a synchronicity!

Pavarotti School

Holley Gene and I went out to a new restaurant in Ventura named "Macaroni Grill". We were treated to Italian music during our meal, and, at one point, our waitress sang an opera song *a cappella* (without musical accompaniment). Her name was Julia and she was very good!

Julia wanted to become an opera singer. Her dream was to go to Italy and study opera at the Pavarotti School.

In order to apply to the school, Julia needed to send them a demo CD of herself singing.

Holley Gene and I have a modest recording studio in our home. We invited Julia over and recorded her singing several songs *a cappella*.

That was the last time we saw or heard from Julia until a few months later, when we received her post card from Italy(!)

Sister Alma

Rose Parenti played the piano at a church Holley Gene and I started going to in Ventura.

We learned later that Rose used to play accordion on the Jack Benny radio show.

As Holley Gene and I continued going to that church, we were asked to put on special performances at Christmas time, Easter, and the like – which we agreed to do.

Rose was getting a little older, so we gradually took over playing piano (me) and organ (Holley Gene) at the church.

One day I got a phone call from Rose. She needed to send in a 'demo tape' for some sort of competition.

I agreed to come to her house and record Rose playing her organ.

Never heard much more about any of this.

Then, one day, we learned about the release of a new Whoopi Goldberg movie, *Sister Act*.

Guess who played Sister Alma in the movie? Sister Alma was the nun who played for Whoopi's choir.

It was Rose Parenti.

More exclamation marks (!!!)

Holley Gene and I played for a church in downtown Ventura for several years. Don Welsh was the minister.

There was one black man in the congregation. He (Eugene) attended church every week. We became the best of friends.

Gene was an accomplished blues keyboardist and liked jazz. One time, he took me to see legendary Stratocaster guitarist Albert Collins at a local theater.

One Christmas season, Holley Gene and I put together a Christmas play for the church's children to perform. We needed a doll baby ('baby Jesus') for 'Mary' and 'Joseph' to carry down the aisle.

We had a photo of Eugene as an infant, dressed in a beautiful white dress. They dressed baby boys like girls back then to thwart kidnappers – who valued boy babies more than girl babies!

Holley Gene took the photo to a craft store in nearby Simi Valley, California. This store specialized in bisque and porcelain doll heads.

Yep, they made a little ebony doll's head that looked just like 'baby Eugene.'

Holley Gene put the head on a doll's body and finished the doll.

Mary and Joseph carried their baby Jesus down the church aisle, the baby carefully wrapped in 'swaddling clothes'.

After the performance, Rev. Don (who was 'in' on what we were doing) addressed the congregation. Of course, Eugene was in attendance.

I forget exactly what Rev. Don said, but it was something

like "This Christmas we honor the Christ child born in each one of us." Afterwards, 'Mary' walked back up the aisle and presented the Baby Jesus to Eugene.

When Gene unwrapped the swaddling clothes from around the doll, you could have heard a pin drop! 'Jesus' was black – and looked like baby Eugene.

There wasn't a dry eye in the house!

Gene made a living making wallet cards for recovering alcoholics and just about any other cause. He eventually moved up to Humboldt County in northern California, became an 'officiant' for local weddings, and played keyboard at the local Masonic lodge.

I lost my friend, Eugene, recently, but have gotten to know his son, Mark, pretty well. Mark is a talented singer-songwriter and specializes in what I'll call 'Christian Rap'.

My Sisters Barbara and Peggy

Barbara, born when I was 4, still lives in our hometown, Middletown, Ohio. She married Dan, a man I admire.

Barb (and Dan) took care of our mother in her later years. After Mother passed away, Barb and Dan took care of our younger sister Peggy. My little sister, Peggy (Margaret Ann), was born when I was 12. Peggy had Down's syndrome and could not live on her own. She was a very special person and a blessing to my family.

I did a special orchestral arrangement and recording of "Climb Ev'ry Mountain" for her because she loved music so much.

Peggy passed away in 2007.

I sometimes feel guilty about not being there to help with Mom and Peggy. But my jobs were out here in California – and I had to provide for my family.

For many years, Barb taught classes to people wishing to complete the requirements for a high school diploma. She also taught some ESL (English second language) classes. Most classes were given at St. Paul's Church in Middletown.

Barbara also plays piano for church every week.

I couldn't have asked for a better sister and brother-in-law!

The Pearl Story

Holley Gene and I took a cruise to the Caribbean. What happened there was another synchronicity.

As we disembarked at various ports of call, passengers were routed through a concourse – a 'gauntlet' of shops selling products of the island and just about everything else under the sun.

One of these was a jewelry shop. And just outside the jewelry shop was a little Down's Syndrome girl, handing out pamphlets. She reminded me of my sister, Peggy.

I asked Holley Gene if we could buy a little piece of jewelry for her.

We asked at the store. They said they knew her and that it would be OK with her mother.

We got her a little necklace and she was very happy! It might even have been her first piece of jewelry.

"Now, here's the rest of the story."

The next stop on our southern Caribbean tour was Isla Margarita (Little Pearl), an island just off the coast of Venezuela.

As we were exiting one of the churches there, we noticed a street vendor just outside the church.

He had a large abalone shell full of loose pearls. There were two black pearls in the shell.

Holley Gene asked him, "How much are the black pearls?"

The street vendor picked up the larger black pearl and handed it to Holley Gene.

"It's yours", he said.

He refused our offers to pay him *something*.

Amazed, we walked back to the ship.

We found out later that it was the custom of the people on the island to give away something early in the new year, for good karma and a prosperous year.

Later, Holley Gene and I realized that she got the free pearl because of good 'karma' from our gift to the little Down's Syndrome girl at an earlier port.

Are you ready for what's coming?

It wasn't until I was writing about this that I realized —

- Down's Syndrome girl
- Isla Margarita (little pearl, also little Margaret)
- My sister Peggy also had Down's Syndrome. Peggy's name was Margaret!

Another synchronicity!

Son Chris

My son, Chris, when he was still in school, had the biggest paper route in Thousand Oaks, CA.

We had a VW van at the time. I took out the back seat and put in carpet and a bean bag chair.

I would drive Chris around his route. He'd sit in the bean

bag chair and 'rubber band' his papers. In rainy weather, he'd put them in plastic bags. We opened the sliding rear door to the van so he could throw the papers out onto the customers' driveways. Neat, huh.

Chris has his own grandchildren now. He's General Foreman for a large painting contractor. They paint big projects like the Ontario (CA) International Airport and four new tilt-up buildings on the old Fisher Body site in Van Nuys, CA.

Daughter Heather

My daughter, Heather, has been an RDA (Registered Dental Assistant) for nearly 30 years.

I was her 'practice guinea pig' years ago when she was preparing for her state exams and certification. I had really shiny teeth back then!

I have written several books of music. *Angel Music* has six original songs in it. One is "Crystal Iridescence". Another original melody is "Cherub'in". Is it a coincidence that Heather's two daughters, born after these songs were written, are named 'Crystal' and 'Melody'?

Over The Rainbow

We all know this song from the 1939 movie, *The Wizard of Oz*.

The song has always had a special place in my heart, having grown up seeing it several times in a movie theater, then on TV - and later, seeing the stage production of *Wicked*.

The song has even more significance to me personally.

A few years ago, Heather was diagnosed with a life-threatening condition.

She underwent surgery, chemotherapy, and radiation treatments at UCLA and Cedars-Sinai hospitals in Los Angeles. Today she is a survivor and doing well. Praise God!

What I didn't know was that my sister, Barbara, back in Ohio, had put Heather's name on the prayer list in the church where I grew up.

I wanted to do something special to thank the congregation for their thoughts and prayers.

I was planning to return to my hometown to attend a high school reunion. I asked if I could play some special music during the church's Sunday service when I was there.

Before we were to leave for Ohio, Holley Gene and I went to an art show on one of the local beaches here in California. A photographer there was selling black and white photos. One of them silhouetted a tree on the shoreline, all in black and white, except for a full-color rainbow overhead. I bought the right to reproduce his image and had some wallet cards made. Along the top of the image, I added the words, "With God, nothing is impossible."

As I played my arrangement of "Over the Rainbow" in church that Sunday morning, the ushers passed out these wallet cards to everyone in the congregation as a 'thank you'.

Guess who made the wallet cards for me (at no charge) – my friend Eugene.

My arrangement starts out with "Twinkle, Twinkle, Little Star," representing my daughter as I remember her as a little girl. Then it enters into a recognizable simple rendition of "Over the Rainbow," representing her as growing up. The bridge changes keys to represent her becoming a woman in her teenage years – then, goes into the most wonderful expression of the song that I am able to play – representing her as the beautiful, mature woman she is today.

103

"Now, here's the rest of the story."

After returning home, Holley Gene and I were watching *Jeopardy* on TV. One of the trivia answers was "The state motto of Ohio".

I was startled to discover that the state motto of Ohio is, "With God, all things are possible."

I had no idea that's what it was – and I had been born and raised there!

Daughter Nicolle

My youngest daughter, Nicolle (yes, that's right, two 'L's), has been an oral surgery assistant for over 20 years. She has worked for several maxillofacial surgeons, one of whom, Dr. James Tamborello, is internationally known. Dr. T. is also a very talented jazz saxophonist.

In 2006, her son (my grandson) Tyler appeared on the scene. What a delight he is! Tyler has my middle name – Francis – just like his Uncle Chris.

Tyler's birthdate is one of the combinations I used at a SCIF.

Arlington Theater Organ

Holley Gene and I started going to the First Christian Church in Santa Paula, CA - a small town near Ventura.

The pastor there at the time, Dr. Phillip McKinley, previously had a church in Santa Barbara, CA. While he was there, he worked with a team of others to restore the theater organ at Santa Barbara's Arlington Theater.

It's a fantastic theater organ! It has all the bells and whistles (literally) anyone could possibly want. It even has a piano up in one of the several overhead 'instrument chambers' that can be played from the organ's keyboard (from the organ's 'manual' in organ lingo). What a thrill it must be to 'ride' the organ console as it comes up from the basement to the stage!

I'm telling you all this because once a month, the Arlington opens its doors to the restoration team and allows them to come in and play the organ.

One Saturday, we took a bus full of church members and their kids to the Arlington to hear Dr. Phil play.

While we were there, Phil invited Holley Gene to play. I even got a chance to play, too.

Dare To Be Great

As God meant it to be, the future is in the hands of our children.

DTBG.org was one of several websites I created for churches, charities, and the like.

The website tells of three outstanding young people.

It also tells of other young people who have been inspired by these three and have since made noteworthy achievements in their lives.

Encourage the young people you know to do the same. They don't have to be nationally recognized. They can excel by performing at their best level.

That's all we should expect them to do – their best.

The Two Foot Hill

One of my 'funnest' things is Ventura's Two Foot Hill.

Yeah, no kidding – that's what I've told all our grandkids and people visiting us in Ventura.

I'd say, "Do you wanna go see the two foot hill? C'mon, I'll take you there."

I drive them down Loma Vista Road, by Ventura College to Ashwood Avenue. Then I turn onto Ashwood heading (where else?) uphill. A couple of blocks uphill on Ashwood, you'll see the sign.

To Foothill (Blvd.)

Get's 'em every time!

The Royal Family

Holley Gene's granddaughter, Chloe, a beautiful young woman inside and out, recently wed her fiancé, Glen.

Here's the story.

Prince William and Princess Kate from England recently visited southern California. During their stay, Prince William played polo in the Santa Barbara area.

Chloe's fiancé, Glen, played against the prince.

After the match, Chloe and Glen got some 'face time' with the prince and princess.

Glen told Prince William that he and Chloe were planning to wed soon. The prince offered Glen some advice, words to the effect that, "Just let her do what she wants with the wedding plans. You'll be happier that way" (not his exact words).

A few months later, on Cinqo de Mayo (the 5th of May), Chloe and Glen were married – at the polo grounds.

You see, Glen's paternal grandparents own the polo grounds.

Another interesting fact is that Chloe's wedding dress was also her mother Carrie's wedding dress – and 51 years ago, her grandmother, Holley Gene's, wedding dress.

Chloe and Glen exchanging their vows.

Holley Gene
in the same dress 51 years earlier.

It was a beautiful wedding – and Glen's grandparents are wonderful people.

There's a little more to the story.

Holley Gene recently started taking physical therapy for backaches. She showed the PT facility receptionist photos from the wedding.

The receptionist said, "Wait. I know her. That's Chloe. She and I used to work together."

Guess what the receptionist's name is – Chloe!

Photo Found At Church

I mentioned earlier that we go to church in Santa Paula, CA, twelve miles from our home.

One day, Holley Gene and several other ladies volunteered to go through the archives of the 110 yr. old church.

They sat down at several of the tables in Harrington Hall, the separate social function building in back of the church, and spread out the various archived materials. Their first objective was to do a loose categorization – photos, letters, newspaper articles, etc.

Each of the ladies picked up some folders to go through.

Holley Gene came to a folder containing old photographs. The first photo in the folder was of some children dressed in clothes of the 50s.

The next photo: "Oh, my gosh! Here's a picture of my mother!"

The photo was of several men and women around a table with a sign on it that said, "NHS 30".

Long story short: It was a photo of the 30th reunion of the graduating high school class of Needles, CA. The photo was taken in Needles.

At the time, Holley Gene's folks lived in northern California. They would have traveled to Needles for the reunion and the photo.

What was this photo doing in Santa Paula?

*Holley Gene's mother, Schatzie,
is in the front row, 2nd from left.*

Later investigation revealed that one of the attendees in the photo (back row, middle) had been the minister at our Santa Paula church in '61.

Holley Gene looked through her mother's senior high school yearbook and found a picture of the minister. His photo was just above Holley Gene's mother in the yearbook, because both their last names started with an 'H'.

What are the odds of all this happening 61 years later? Plus the fact that Holley Gene 'just happened' to look through the photos that contained her mother's photo – and that she even noticed.

Yes! Another synchronicity!!! We don't know the message it has for us, yet.

Holley Gene says, "Miracles happen all the time. The real miracle is that we notice them."

We have been given divine examples, analogies and synchronicities to teach us and to help us understand our own life's journey. Some of them:

> A caterpillar enters its cocoon having never seen a butterfly - yet emerges as a butterfly.

> After the dreariness endured during the cold winter months, there is always rebirth in the Spring.

> The sun, moon, and stars gave man something to think about – other than just his survival needs.

It is my belief that everything on this earth is connected – and that all is in Divine Order, as planned by God or whoever you believe is the Creator.

Prepare to be amazed!

An Italian mathematician, Leonardo Fibonacci (pronounced 'fee-bow-<u>nah</u>-chee'), is known for a number sequence named the Fibonacci series.

The structure of the Fibonacci series is made as follows.

Start with 0 and 1:

0,1

Now add these two numbers, and put the sum on the right:

0,1,1

Now add the rightmost two numbers and put the sum on the right:

0,1,1,2

Again, add the rightmost two numbers and put the sum on the right:

0,1,1,2,3

Continue doing this. I have carried the series out for you to 17 places:

0, 1, 1, 2, 3, 5, 8, 13, 21, 34, 55, 89, 144, 233, 377, 610, 987, ...

The numbers in the series are called *Fibonacci numbers.*

Now, divide the rightmost number by its predecessor. For example, in the long sequence shown above, divide 987 by 610. The 'answer' (the 'quotient', the 'ratio') is approximately 1.6, known as the *Divine Ratio.*

Stick with me on this.
You will not believe what's coming!

The Divine Ratio is found everywhere in nature and in everyone of us on the planet!

Here are some examples.

On many plants, the number of petals is a Fibonacci number:

- buttercups have 5 petals. 5 is a number in the Fibonacci series;
- lilies and irises have 3 petals. 3 is a Fibonacci number;
- daisies can be found with 34, 55 or even 89 petals (all Fibonacci numbers).
- a large sunflower can have 55 and 89 spirals of seeds (again, Fibonacci numbers).
- Fibonacci numbers can be found in pine cones, cauliflower, broccoli, lettuce, bananas, apples, etc.

Better sit down before you read further!

Measure the lengths of the bones in your finger (best seen by slightly bending the finger). The ratio of the length of the longest bone in your finger to the middle bone is approximately 1.6, the Divine Ratio!

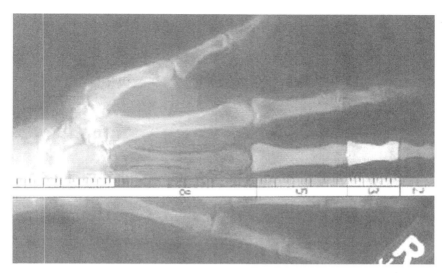

This is true for the fingers of everyone in the world!

In the picture above, note that the lengths of the bones in the finger are all Fibonacci numbers (2, 3, 5, 8)!

There's even more unbelievable stuff coming!

As the animal living in the spiral-shaped Nautilus sea shell grows, it adds internal chambers to the shell. In each new turn added to the spiral, the shell grows by the amount of the Divine Ratio!

In the most pleasing rectangles to the eye, so-called 'golden' rectangles, the ratio of length to width is the Divine Ratio. In the Parthenon, built on the top of the Acropolis hill in Athens, the spaces between the columns form 'golden' rectangles.

Leonardo DaVinci used the Divine Ratio in his paintings, including the famous "Mona Lisa".

The Great Pyramid of Giza, Egypt, 4,600 years old, was built long before the Greeks. Its dimensions are also based on the Divine Ratio.

Are you beginning to believe that all is in Divine Order?

Space and Time Travel

We, as well as all other creatures on this earth, have learned to live within the three dimensions of space and the dimension of time.

In 1913, Niels Bohr was the first to propose a model of the atoms that make up our universe. His model, familiar to all students, has a nucleus (a center) with electrons in orbit around the nucleus.

We have since learned that the electrons actually orbit the nucleus in a 'cloud' that, statistically speaking, can extend well beyond the nucleus. It is possible (not very probable) that some of your electrons' orbits can extend beyond the confines of your visible body.

I say 'visible' because we're used to seeing the extent of how our bodies occupy space (say, to the end of your big toe). In fact, some of our electrons could be way out there somewhere (for example, across the street). If that's true, our 'intrinsic' body could extend across the street, too.

Traveling Back in Time

Let's say that someday, we will actually be capable of sending someone back in time 5 minutes.

DO NOT VOLUNTEER TO DO THIS!

One reason: if you do travel in time, will all the electrons of your 'intrinsic' body go with you?(!)

Here's perhaps a more important reason -

Picture this scenario. You're lying on a time machine's table as the volunteer to be the first to go back in time 5 minutes.

The test conductor approaches the control panel and pushes the button to make it all happen.

Let's say it worked.

You wouldn't know that it worked!

Because 5 minutes in the past you'd be lying on the time machine's table, as the volunteer to be the first to go back in time 5 minutes.

The test conductor would again approach the control panel and push the button (again) to make it all happen.

You wouldn't know that it worked (again)!

Because you'd be lying on the time machine's table, as the volunteer to be the first to go back in time 5 minutes.

The test conductor would (again) approach the control panel and push the button (again) to make it all happen.

THIS IS WHAT YOU'LL BE DOING UNTIL HELL FREEZES OVER!

If you <u>do</u> volunteer to go back in time, don't elect to go back too far.

For example, if you volunteered to go back to Civil War times, you wouldn't have existed back then!

Traveling to the Future

What would be the scenario if someone could actually travel into the future?

Let's say that the day after tomorrow, you'll be hit by a bus and killed.

Don't go too far into the future because you might not be there!

So much for human curiosity!

My Blessings

The Creator has blessed me with:

- life
- love
- family
- friends

and an awareness of the miracles around me

I am truly thankful for these, for what they have taught me.

Thoughts I Leave With You

- Pursue all your interests – especially those that excite you.
- Do the best you can.
- Love and help one another.
- Seek to remember what you already know.

Honor and give thanks to the Creator. Know that each of us is a facet of 'The Great Gem'.

NOW is the only time we have. Live and love in the now.

Life is not measured by the number of breaths we take, but by the moments that take our breath away.

And at the last -

> unhesitatingly

>   enter that realm

>   where all living creatures go

>   . . . knowing you are loved.

Don't spend your life in a secluded SCIF.

See the synchronicities in your life,
and accept the gifts they bring. . .